MONEY MADNESS

MONEY MADNESS
STRANGE MANIAS AND EXTRAORDINARY SCHEMES ON AND OFF WALL STREET

John M. Waggoner

BUSINESS ONE IRWIN
Homewood, IL 60430

Executive editor: Jeffrey A. Krames
Project editor: Jane Lightell
Production manager: Carma W. Fazio
Cover Design: Renee Klyczek Nordstrom
Compositor: Carlisle Communications, Ltd.
Typeface: 11/13 Century Schoolbook
Printer: Arcata Graphics/Kingsport

Library of Congress Cataloging-in-Publication Data

Waggoner, John M.
    Money madness : strange manias and extraordinary schemes on and
off Wall Street / John M. Waggoner.
      p.   cm.
    ISBN 1–55623–290–X
    1. Investments—United States—History. 2. Speculation—History.
I. Title.
HG4910.W25 1990
332.6′0973—dc20   90–47935

Printed in the United States of America

1 2 3 4 5 6 7 8 9 0 AGK 7 6 5 4 3 2 1 0

For Yvonne
When I had no wings to fly, you flew to me
And for Nathaniel and Hope
Blessings beyond my wildest dreams

PREFACE

It's customary for an author to acknowledge in the preface the debts owed to him, and it's equally customary for a first time author to do so at embarrassing length. So who am I to break tradition?

I owe a great deal to the many people who not only put up with me while I was assembling this book but who helped me along the way. First and foremost, of course, is my wife, Yvonne Surette, who not only tolerated my late hours, but proved to be one of the best and ablest critics of my manuscripts. Without her there would have been no book and, quite likely, no author, either; I probably would have met a sudden end while absentmindedly working some small electrical appliance.

I could write a small book on the many miracles wrought by Jeffrey Seglin, my longtime friend and frequent benefactor. I don't know a more talented writer or more patient editor. Jeffrey suggested that I write this book, put me in touch with Jeffrey Krames, his editor at BUSINESS ONE IRWIN, as well as his agent, Evan Marshall. His comments on the manuscript were a wonderful help to me and his care and encouragement a true blessing.

Most people credit their parents with giving them love, help, and inspiration; mine not only did that but critiqued my manuscript and—in a true display of devotion—allowed me to inhabit an upstairs room and use their computer. My father, Miles Waggoner, went painstakingly through my draft; his comments are the work of the greater craftsman. My stepmother, Mary Waggoner, did the same, and the book is far better for that. My mother, Dorothy Mundinger, read the manuscript as well, and her comments, love, and support were a great help.

I also owe a large debt to my good friend and neighbor, Scott Holmes, who read my manuscript through several laborious versions and gave me some of the sharpest feedback and insights into the writing. His comments on the section on Daniel Drew and the Erie Railroad scandal were invaluable.

Finally, I'd like to thank Jim Henderson and Pat Walkup, my editors at *USA Today,* who gave me time to work on the book, put up with me while in the throes of working on it, and taught me a great deal about writing, as well. In addition, I need to thank my editor, Jeffrey Krames, for not coming after me with an ax, as well as for his numerous contributions to getting this work in print.

As a final note, I'd be greatly remiss in not acknowledging a large debt to the spirit of William Cuppy in the illustrative sections at the end of each chapter. His work, *The Decline and Fall of Practically Everybody,* is the best history book ever written; and if you liked my poor efforts at footnoting, you'll love the work of the master. If you haven't read Cuppy, you haven't read history.

John M. Waggoner

CONTENTS

INTRODUCTION

"Do you sincerely want to be rich?"

For most people, the answer to this question, first posed by con artist and mutual fund huckster extraordinaire Bernie Cornfeld, is remarkably simple. It's like asking, "Do you sincerely want to be happy?" "Do you sincerely want to breathe?" "Do you sincerely want to avoid being used as a volleyball by polar bears?"

Therein lies the root of money madnesses. Most people are reasonably sane, and the average person is tolerably honest. But when the chance to make a tidy sum with relatively little risk comes along, prudence is often the first casualty. The twitch of fiscal insanity can come in a mass movement, such as a bull market in stocks, or in individual doses, such as small-time scams. In either event, no one is immune.

You might think from reading the headlines in most newspapers that financial fiascos are unique to the 1980s. And, indeed, there's been a financial full moon over America for most of the last decade, with billions of dollars squandered in nearly every way imaginable. The savings and loan crisis, for example, has become so huge that the numbers involved become unreal, like the distance between

Pasadena and the Crab Nebula. At last count, thrifts have lost some $200 billion, and that might be a conservative estimate. To put that into some perspective, if the government forced you to cough up one buck every second, it would get $1 million out of you in 11.6 days. If you handed the tax man a bat hide every second for 31.7 years, the government would be $1 billion richer. To get to $200 billion, you, your heirs and assignees would have to give Uncle Sam a sawbuck a second for 6,340 years.

With such numbers screaming out of the newspapers daily, most people have become accustomed to multimillion, or multibillion, incidents of economic idiocy. How did our national pastime become making and losing money? Well, there were extenuating circumstances for the 1980s, just like there were for the Hundred Years' War. The primary cause of the foolishness in the 1980s were the 1970s, which—as Gary Trudeau, the creator of Doonesbury, put it— really were a kidney stone of a decade. For example, between 1977 and midyear 1982, the cost of living rose 60 percent. By comparison, inflation rose 64 percent for the entire decade of the 80s, and much of that rise came in 1980 and 1981. Interest rates, fueled by the tight-money policies of the indomitable Paul Volcker, chairman of the Federal Reserve, rose to over 16 percent on three-month Treasury bills.

Financial markets reflected the economic landscape in the 1970s. The Dow Jones Industrial Average, for example, lost about 40 percent of its value in the bear market of 1973 to 1974, and long-term investors earned only about 80 percent over the entire decade—somewhat less than a passbook savings account. After inflation, any gains were probably completely illusory. The bond market also went straight into the tank, as investors learned the age-old axiom of the bond market: When interest rates rise, bond prices fall. Even money-market mutual funds, the premier investment of the early part of the 1980s, lost a good chunk of their double-digit yields to inflation.

So by the time the 1980s rolled around, the nation was in the mood for making money. The decade started with a huge rise in the price of gold, the first major market to rise and then collapse in flames. Housing prices followed gold's upward spiral, as did a bull market in stocks of epic proportions. By the mid-1980s, money was the infatuation of the nation.

As anyone with a pulse knows, the real estate and securities markets followed gold back down. While there are still some healthy pockets in the real estate markets, most of them are in places like Cleveland. You can make good money there, but when you wake up in the morning, you're still in Cleveland. Stocks wrote themselves into the history books in 1987, although they later recovered.

If you're feeling a bit chagrined about having lived through such a foolish period, don't be. Money manias weren't just one of those wacky fads of the 1980s, like dwarf bowling and Republicanism. This country's fondness for cash has led it into several well-known outbreaks of money mania throughout its history.

And it's no wonder. The ability to grab a money-making opportunity when it's around was one of reasons listed in the Declaration of Independence for breaking from Great Britain: the pursuit of happiness. This is often given (wrongly) as a reason for doing something really stupid, like abandoning your wife and kids for a religious cult in Borneo. *Happiness,* however, meant something different in Thomas Jefferson's day: It meant, roughly, *luck,* or *fortune.* The meaning survives, mostly in the negative form, in words like *mishap* and *hapless.* The colonists didn't like the fact that the king considered most things in the ground, and in commerce, to belong to him.

The result was not only the union, but also this country's propensity towards rushing like lemmings to the lure of money. Even before the United States was founded, early settlers had a penchant for grabbing a quick buck. The country was settled by men and women who were not only looking for a new life, but gold and riches as well. The advertisements of the day that would lure settlers to the new land as often as not promised gold, silver, and jewels lying about on the beaches, there for the taking.

Some money manias, such as the great Crash of 1929, have been seared into the country's memory. Many better writers, historians, and economists have tried their hand at explaining the great Crash, and it's not the purpose of this book to illuminate the better-known fiscal fiascos of history. The purpose is, instead, to look at some of the lesser-known manias that have swept across the land and, eventually, faded from general knowledge.

For example, although most people are familiar with the forty-niners and the California gold rush, the North Carolina gold rush, the nation's first, has all but faded into obscurity. Even so, it was the model for all the gold rushes that followed it and, more than likely, similar to most that preceeded it. And the echoes of the gold rush haven't settled yet; as early as this year, mining companies were exploring old gold fields in North and South Carolina, hoping to bring gold from the detritus of the old mines.

Land, too, was a great lure for the early settlers, and it has endured to this day as the single most important facet of the American dream. Then, as now, people were willing to stake their entire fortunes on the future of a cow pasture. Back then, however, cow pastures were far less scarce—but people in the 1830s were more than willing to bet the farm on them. Even the Father of our Country, George Washington, was infected with land fever; and the people who live in Washington, D.C., today owe their location on 10 square miles of swampland to the location of Washington's prime real estate.

By the 1860s, the stock market had come into its own, and the events that occurred in postwar Wall Street would make even the most hardened trader of today blush—if not with shame, then with envy. Back then, when a million dollars was really worth something, a select band of men thought nothing of tossing millions onto the Street, provided they had the inside knowledge that it was a sure thing.

Skipping forward to the 1920s, stocks were again the investment of choice. Everyone may not know, however, that the mutual fund was having its first real heyday. Although the funds were good for the people who ran them, they proved to be somewhat less so for those who bought them. They were, in fact, one of the greatest scandals in a scandal-ridden market.

Land also became attractive in the 1920s, and Florida land became positively ravishing. Investors poured billions of mostly borrowed money into the "American Riviera," only to see it sink back into swampland. And what the hucksters didn't grab, the hurricane of 1926 blew into Biscayne Bay.

Individual investors weren't entirely to blame for all the fiscal fiascos of the last 200-odd years. In fact, one of the greatest comforts of studying financial history is the discovery that it was often the "smart money" that was taken in first, last, and in between. In the early 1960s, for example, a two-bit soybean oil middleman in Bayonne, New Jersey, took the American Express Company, the New York Stock Exchange, and numerous major banks to the cleaners. The result—combined with the assassination of John F. Kennedy—was the steepest one-day drop in common stock share prices in history.

Throughout all of this were all the small-time scams and con artists who have taken a peculiarly revered place in American history. Con artists and flimflams are always with us, but they come into particular focus when the scent of money is in the air. And Americans have always had a soft spot in their hearts for the medicine men, the traveling flimflam artists, and the P. T. Barnums of the world. In the early days of the Republic, those who made their livings by their wits were just as revered as those who carved a livelihood out of the raw wilderness. The rightness or wrongness of 'the situation didn't seem to have anything to do with it. The flimflam man has become a part of the lore of American history and a large part of the lore of money manias.

In money manias and outright frauds, of course, you can stand to lose a great deal of money. In order to make money, however, you have to take certain risks. Although the main aim of this book is to entertain and amuse, there's some useful instruction here, too. By looking at history, you can not only find out how people are stupid with their cash, you can discover how to avoid being stupid with yours. And that can be one of the best lessons of all.

CHAPTER 1

NORTH CAROLINA GOLD

The first English settlers to North Carolina came lured, at least in part, by the promise of gold. The settlers were told about the gold by the promoters of the venture, who, in turn, had heard it from Spanish explorers. The Spanish had heard it from the Indians.

When the Spanish first poked about the New World, the Indians took note of their superior weaponry as well as their general know-it-all bossiness. "We sailed all the way over from a faraway place," they would say, gesturing with their guns.

The Indians nodded.

"We came to claim this land for our king and queen," the Spanish said.

The Indians nodded again.

"Do you know where we could find gold?"

The Indians pointed west. "That way," they said.

Unfortunately for the Indians, the Spanish stayed anyway.

Of course, the Spanish always thought the Indians were telling the truth and told each other that gold was out west somewhere. At that time, "west" was the East Coast. This could be one reason why so many people seemed to be lost in those days. Nevertheless, one thing led to another, and, through a series of predictable misunderstandings a few decades later, Sir Walter Raleigh came to believe the Indians had been pointing to North Carolina. He was wrong.

In one of those strange quirks of history, there actually was gold in North Carolina—and throughout the Southeast, since gold was found from Maryland to Alabama. There was enough gold, in fact, to spark the first gold rush in American history. As it turned out, North Carolina was full of enough gold to make it the nation's foremost gold producer until the California gold rush of 1849. As is often the case when gold is discovered, a few profited from the discovery, and many more didn't. While other gold strikes were richer, and better documented, the North Carolina gold rush was the model for all the gold rushes that came after. In short, it was a mess.

It took a fair amount of time for gold-seekers just to find North Carolina. Raleigh did manage to send a group of settlers there, and they established a small colony on the North Carolina coast near Roanoake. The new settlers had many hopes and aspirations, among which was finding gold.

Sir Walter died some years later, when an ax fell on his neck. Compared to what his settlers got, he was probably lucky. Roanoake is a delightful place to spend a vacation but a really rotten place to start a colony. The land there is mostly sand, and the mosquitoes are as persistent as insurance salesmen. The area also has an unfortunate tendency to disappear during hurricanes, which occur with annoying frequency.

The first group of settlers came to Roanoake in 1585, stayed a year, and then decided that England wasn't such a bad place after all. They left just in time to miss a group of ships that Raleigh had sent to resupply the colony. Those colonists left, too. Raleigh wasn't one to miss a chance at establishing the first English colony in the New World, so he sent another group packing to America in May 1587. The first colonists didn't find gold. They didn't find Virginia either, which was their original destination. The captain of the ship dropped them off at Roanoake, muttering something about a previous engagement elsewhere. After two years, no one could find the settlement, and it became known as "The Lost Colony."

Despite the failure of the Roanoke colony, North Carolina was settled anyway, due mainly to sheer persistance. People had not been settling North Carolina for a long time, starting in 1526, when Lucas Vasquez de Ayllon of Spain established a colony on Cape Fear. It didn't take. After Ayllon, de Soto went though looking for gold. He missed the gold lying about in the streambeds and contented himself with discovering the Mississippi. After Raleigh's attempt at colonizing the area, Sir Robert Heath gave it a shot. He didn't have any better luck than the rest.

Eventually, settlers dribbled in from Virginia, trying to escape the congestion in Jamestown. They kept moving further south, and before they knew it they were in North Carolina. Early settlers of the area did ask the local Indians if there was any gold in the area. The Indians took a look at the new settlers and shook their heads regretfully. There was, they said, plenty of gold "out west" and gave helpful directions.

No one found gold until 1799, when young Conrad Reed, a farmer's son in Cabarrus county, was playing around in Meadow Creek, the stream that ran behind his father's barn. As he was playing, he found an unusually heavy rock, about the size of a shoe. It had an appealing yellow color and caught the light nicely, so he brought it home. His father, John Reed, took the rock to the local silversmith, who assured him it had no value. John used it as a doorstop for the next three years.

Reed wasn't convinced that the rock was worthless, and took it with him on a trip to Fayetteville. The local jeweler took a look at it. "John, it's gold!", the man said. He took another look at the rock. He took a look at John. "It's worth— ummm—by God, John, it must be worth $3.00 —no, $3.50!"

John Reed thought $3.50 was a fine price for a 17-pound gold nugget. To celebrate his good luck, Reed bought some coffee beans, which the store clerk assured him were from South America. His wife, who had never seen coffee beans before, cooked them up with pork the next night for supper. It was a bad day all around for Reed.

Word eventually leaked out, however, that the jeweler had sold the nugget for several thousand dollars. John may have been slow, but he wasn't stupid. He went back to the jeweler, and, quite possibly, offered to trade some lead with the jeweler for the gold. He rode back more amply rewarded for the sale.

Reed then went back for a second look at his stream and filled a quart jar with yellow nuggets. Meadow Creek, it seems, was just loaded with gold. Eventually, one of his slaves found a nugget weighing 28 pounds.

John Reed had discovered an area rich in gold, and—for a few brief years in the early part of the 1800s—he was the richest man in North Carolina. This wasn't saying a lot, but it was something. He formed a company with some partners and began mining operations in Meadow Creek. The holes they dug along Meadow Creek are still visible today, particularly during flood season.

Reed's neighbors noticed, naturally, that he was living pretty well. Soon anyone with any gumption was out in the streambeds, panning for gold. By 1829, a real boom was under way. Local papers of the day carried headlines such as "Number of Gold Mines Increasing Every Day," "Farmers Find Gold in Every Hill," "Moneyed Men from Every Quarter of the Union Purchasing Land at Extravagant Prices," and "Gold Digging Amounts to Mania."

The early mines in North Carolina weren't a bit like the kinds that probably come to mind. Part of this has to do with the way gold is scattered across the South, which is rather different from the way gold is scattered across most of the world. For example, in the great gold and silver strikes of California and Nevada, the ore ran in fairly regular, straight veins, or lodes, through rock. If you were lucky enough to find a gold or silver vein in the West, you could generally follow it for some distance until it petered out or went too deep for you to follow.

North Carolina gold was different. Much of the gold there was in shallow deposits, or placers, sprinkled about a long, narrow "gold belt" that stretched across the Piedmont—the coastal plain stretching roughly from Washington, D.C., to northwest Alabama between the Appalachian mountains and the Atlantic ocean. The distribution pattern of the gold was erratic, to say the least—as if some benevolent giant had spread a fistful of gold nuggets across the lower half of the East Coast.

If the area hadn't been interlaced with streams and creeks, the gold placers would have been extremely difficult to find, and it's doubtful there would have been much of a gold rush. Over the course of the years, however, streams meandered across gold placers. The water would gradually erode the gold, filling select areas of the streambed with gold dust, and occasionally revealing gold nuggets of the kind that Conrad Reed found.

Sometimes prospectors would find an entire placer, a nest of gold dust and nuggets just under the surface of the ground. When this happened, they would either take their gold, convert it to cash, and live a life of quiet luxury, or they would get drunk, squander it all on a few moments of self-indulgence, and then drag in partners to lose the rest of their money. In most cases, the latter course of action prevailed.

With gold rushes, people tend to go for the easiest to reach. There's no sense in digging a mine, after all, if you can get rich without digging one. And, at least at first, there was plenty of gold lying around in stream beds in North Carolina. So the first gold rushers concentrated on the prospecting in the streambeds. So the early North Carolina mines were only mines in the sense that some digging was done every once in a while.

Getting gold from a streambed is relatively easy. Basically, you fill a pan with sand and water from a creekbed. After sloshing it around in the pan for a while—and splashing out half the gold—what's left in the bottom of the pan is either gold, which is heavier than most creekbed gunk, or it's sand. If it's gold, you stay put. If it's sand, you move.

There's only room enough for so many prospectors in a creek, however, and streams have a tendency to meander, leaving gold deposits in dried-up streambeds. Some people were smart enough to reason that if there was gold in the streambed, there was probably gold in the banks of the stream as well. Some of these explorations led to placer deposits.

Finding placer deposits is interesting work if you like digging holes. All you have to do is dig holes all over the place, shovel the dirt into a hollowed-out log called a "rocker," add water, rock the dirt and water back and forth until most of the gold spills out, and then look on the bottom. If there's any gold left at the bottom, you stay where you are. If not, you dig more holes.

At least in the early part of the boom, then, most of the "gold mines" were just holes in the ground with rockers next to them. They also didn't exactly prove to be a gold mine for the miners, who, after paying off the landowners, took home about a pennyweight of gold a day. That translated into about 90 cents' worth of gold. Out of that, of course, they had to pay for food, equipment, whiskey, and gambling losses. It wasn't until later, in most cases, that people actually started digging mines.

The lure of gold in the streambeds, however, was enough to cause a sensation. In Burke County, North Carolina, a businessman named Isaac T. Avery wrote to a friend:

> I mentioned in one of my letters the Discovery of Gold in Burke . . . half the citizens of Wilksboro and its vicinity are in Burke, either as actual operatives in Mines, or as speculators buying Gold Lands. A single mine has averaged from $2,000 to $2,500 weekly since the first of April, and I do not hesitate to say, that there will be 2,000 men employed in Burke as Miners by the first of August.

Naturally, the biggest stakes were held by those who could afford to buy and work them—in short, those who already had a great deal of capital and a number of slaves. By 1829, some 5,000 slaves were at work in Burke county, and one can expect there were similar numbers throughout the South doing the same thing. In the meantime, the fields lay fallow.

Not all the laborers were slaves. Lawyers left their offices, doctors abandoned their practices, and farmers left their livestock to pan for gold. Women and children waded into the streams alongside the men, and overnight towns of one- and two-room log huts sprung up beside the streams.

Reports of easy gold spread across the country. Nathaniel Hawthorne, in "Peter Goldthwait's Treasure," noted that the hero had once gone on a prospecting venture: "Once, he had gone on a gold-gathering expedition, somewhere to the South, and ingeniously contrived to empty his pockets more thoroughly than ever; while others, doubtless, were filling theirs with native bullion by the handful."

One such adventurer was a Salem, Massachusetts sea captain named Jonathan Porter Felt, who once worked for Hawthorne's uncle-in-law. Felt, along with several others, bought land in Anson County, North Carolina, in October 1828. After three years of work rocking and panning, they went broke, and sold the land sometime thereafter. It's unlikely that Felt was the only one in the country who had attempted the same thing.

The reason for Felt's failure is that he came too late in the boom for big money to be found in the creekbeds of North Carolina. The days of panning and rocking were coming to a close by 1828, and the days of the mines were to follow. One of the first to propose a mine was William Thornton, who had designed the U.S. Capitol. He, along with Thomas Tudor Tucker, treasurer of the United States, and John Van Ness, president of the Bank of the United States, made several visits to North Carolina. Thornton figured that if there was gold in the streambeds, there was probably gold in the hills nearby. For some reason, he never got back to it.

It wasn't until the late 1820s that someone latched onto William Thornton's idea that the gold might be underground as well as lying near the surface. One Tobias Barringer, a farmer in Stanley County, was panning for gold when he noticed the gold stopped at a certain point in the creek. So he dug a little way into a nearby hill, where he found a vein of gold. He hustled off, found some investors, and started the Barringer Mine, which eventually yielded some $100,000 worth of gold.

Mining in North Carolina was fraught with problems, although several large and prosperous mines flourished there for several decades. The biggest problems was the tendancy of gold veins to meander. In the West, the biggest problem in mining gold was digging far enough down: After a certain point, deep mines either got too hot or filled up with water. In North Carolina, gold veins shoot off at 45-degree angles, disappear for a time, and then reemerge in a different direction.

Many of the early true mines were open trenches that attempted to follow the veins as far as possible without actually going underground. The problem with these, of course, was that a good rainfall could delay operations for days as workers drained them. In due course, true mines with shafts and galleries appeared. Although never as extensive as the mines out west—there was nothing in North Carolina to compare with the Comstock Lode—the North Carolina mines eventually grew into large operations with thousands of workers, labor disputes, cave-ins, and debauched miners

The latter were particularly noted in the contemporary accounts. Gold mining brings out the worst in people, and the North Carolina gold rush was no exception. The Ransome Bridge area, for example, became the model for the later Western gold mining towns. When the miners weren't digging, they liked to drink, gamble, and shoot each other. Fourteen men—all from different states—died in one memorable shootout, and the locals buried them in plots arranged in the shape of the union.

As word of the gold rush got out, miners poured into North Carolina from all over the world, and the entire state began to look like it had been overrun by moles the size of school buses. A writer in 1831 described the scene:

> It is not five years since these mines began to be worked to any considerable extent; indeed it is hardly half that period. And yet many of them are worked on an extensive scale. And mills for grinding the ore, propelled by water or by steam, are erected in vast numbers. One of the [mine owners] . . . told me that their company now employs 600 hands! And he stated that the whole number of men now employed at the mines in the southern states is at least 20,000. . . . The chief miners (I mean laborers) are foreigners— Germans, Swiss, Swedes, Spaniards, Welsh, Scotch, etc. There are no less than thirteen different languages spoken at the mines in this state!

The immigrants, unfortunately, took up the ways of the good folks of Ransome Bridge:

> I am pained to learn that the morals of these miners are deplorably bad. Indeed I can hardly conceive of a more immoral community than exists around these mines. Drunkenness, gambling, fighting, lewdness and every other vice exists here to an awful extent. Many of the men, by working three days in the week, make several dollars, and then devote the remaining four to every species of vice. The colored people—slaves—are generally the most moral.

The gold fever moved south, and the people who caught it didn't get particularly better. It struck especially hard in Georgia. As is often the case, several people claimed to have been the first to find gold there. The most convincing case is for the claims of Benjamin Parks, whose story uncannily mirrors Jed Clampett of *The Beverly Hillbillies*. According to this claim, Parks was a poor mountaineer who was hunting in north Georgia. One day, as he was shooting at some deer, he tripped over a large piece of quartz. He picked up the rock and saw flecks of gold in it.

Parks quickly acquired mineral rights to about 40 acres of land in north Georgia. Once it became clear that

Parks was getting gold from the ground, the owners sued, but to no avail. Parks sold the mineral rights to John C. Calhoun, the Senator, and the workings there became known as the Calhoun mine.

In Georgia, the people the gold rush struck hardest were the Cherokees. This tribe was one of the so-called five civilized tribes of the Southeastern United States, with an admirable governmental and social structure. Some say the Indians were well aware of the gold deposits on their land; others say the Cherokees were more interested in the copper deposits in the area. In any case, they certainly didn't offer the lands to anyone else, although they sometimes gave out rough maps of sure-fire gold deposits just a little further west.

The Cherokees had never been terribly impressed with the caliber of white settlers streaming into their lands, particularly with the Georgians, who were, by and large, the descendants of refugees from the British penal system. The Cherokees had sided with the British during the French and Indian Wars and, after a bit more experience with the colonials, stayed on with the British during the Revolution. After the war, they continued resistance until, in 1791, the U.S. government gave the Cherokees permanent claim to a large hunk of north Georgia.

When it comes to gold, such niceties as treaties and land ownership tend to go by the wayside. In the United States of the 1820s and 1830s, this was particularly true if the land belonged to the Indians. As word of the richness of the gold finds spread, thousands of would-be miners came into the area. William Blake, a mining engineer, wrote in 1859 of what had happened two decades earlier:

> The rush for the mines brought into the country thousands of men of great diversity of character, many of them dissipated and regardless of the future. Shanty groceries were set

up all over the country, where whisky was freely sold, and
mountebanks attended with all kinds of tricks and shows, in
the endeavor to share the easily-gotten gold of the miners.
Drinking, gambling and fighting were rife, and laws were
little known and less cared for. The poor Indians saw their
beautiful hillsides, where they and their fathers had chased
the deer for centuries, occupied by these centers of vice and
immorality, and their lovely valleys and cool dells dug over
and rendered hideous to the sight.

The United States stationed troops around the Cherokees' land to keep miners out, but to little avail. In 1830,
the state of Georgia brought in the Georgia National
Guard, who were every bit as ineffective as the federal
troops. In 1831 and 1832, the state threw up its hands, held
a lottery for the Cherokee lands, and parceled out the
territory in 40-acre lots. The Cherokees were sent "out
west"—to Oklahoma. The relocation was one of the most
brutal forced marches in history. The Cherokees—those
who survived the march—called it the "Trail of Tears." A
few, however, managed to flee to North Carolina, where
their descendants remain today.

With the Indians gone, the gold miners could plunder
the area unhindered. Hard by where Calhoun had started
his mine, a gentleman named Nathaniel Nuckolls set up a
small tavern, which soon became a haven for the miners.
The town that eventually sprang up there became Nuckollsville, which, naturally, became called Knucklesville, because of all the fighting that took place there.

When the Cherokees were officially kicked out, and
their land auctioned off, a family of orphans bought the
area in which Knucklesville was sitting. The town bought
them off and prospered. The population increased, and, by
1833, the town had a newspaper, the *Western Herald*. Eventually, Nuckollsville had about 2,000 inhabitants and
served as the county seat. In an effort to clean up its image,

it changed its name to Auraria, which means "gold mine" in Latin.

A hoary old business adage says that when there's a gold rush, the most money is made by selling picks and shovels. In Auraria's case, the big growth industry was law. The city's role as de facto county seat had something to do with that, but the main reason is that where there's gold, there's plenty of real estate lawsuits. If you can't prove a claim by tenacity or shotgun, you have to resort to law, and plenty of lawyers came to settle in Auraria.

Auraria's time in the sun was brief, however; just to the north, a small town first named Lick Log, then the old Indian name Dahlonega, started its road to ascendancy. When Dahlonega was named the official county seat of Lumpkin County, the lawyers dropped Auraria like a live hand grenade. The Calhoun mine's production started to flag, and the easy gold in the streams near Auraria started to dwindle as well. By the time gold was discovered in California in 1848, Auraria was well on the wane. Today, it's just a couple of houses and a historical marker on Route 9E in north Georgia, one of several ghost towns left by the gold rush.

Dahlonega then became the center of the mining fever in north Georgia, and the United States established a mint and assay office there in 1838. Other branch mints opened up in Charlotte, South Carolina, and New Orleans. The government needed a mint there for several reasons. First of all, Georgia and North Carolina produced little but agricultural products in the early 1800s, and anything else the growing population needed had to be imported from other states. As a result, currency was scarce, and at least one private mint, the Bechtler Mint, was already doing a booming business. The addition of a mint also discouraged the issue of paper notes by private banks, which was to be a considerable problem for several years to come.

By the time the government established its mint, however, the Southern gold rush had already passed its peak. In 1834, North Carolina, South Carolina, Virginia, and Georgia produced 43,299 ounces of gold, a figure never to be equaled again. (At $400 per ounce, where gold is currently selling, that comes out to more than $17 million. Not bad for a year's work.)

Gold fever also spread northward to Virginia, albeit much more slowly. Thomas Jefferson was the first to notice gold in Virginia, having found a lump of gold ore on the north side of the Rappahannock River in 1782. He got 17 pennyweights of gold out of the ore. Jefferson, who died strapped for cash, never followed up on Virginia gold. He had other things to do.

Although Virginians—and, to a minor extent, their neighbors in Maryland—dug up the land with the best of them, gold mining never really caught on north of the Carolinas. A few small mines opened as early as 1828 in Virginia, but they weren't much to look at. A careless dog could have covered most of them up.

The depression of 1836 to 1842 squashed gold production in the South for a time. Normally, you'd figure people would look even harder for gold when times are bad. But that's the pesky thing about depressions. First of all, depressions result in lower prices for just about everything, including gold. So there wasn't as much money in gold after the economy went up the flume.

Secondly, much of the gold lying around for the taking in the region had been taken. By 1836, the real gold producers were the mines, which were expensive to run. When you got gold out of a Southern gold mine, it wasn't a matter of hauling the nuggets out of the ground and melting them down. Instead, you hauled tons of rock up out of the shaft and crushed the rocks. In most cases, this meant you had to buy a rock-crusher, which was usually called a "stamp press." This was a steam-powered behemoth with huge iron stamps that would crush the ore into usable form.

Next, you had to separate the gold from the ore. The best method involved running it through a sublimate of mercury, which extracted the gold and left the rest. One can only imagine how many workers suffered from mercury poisoning during the gold rush period. All of the above equipment was expensive, as were other commodities needed for a serious mining operation, such as pumps for keeping the shafts dry and housing for the laborers. And during the depression of 1836, money simply wasn't to be had, particularly for speculative gold mining ventures.

By 1837, the South's output of gold was 13,644 ounces, or $5.5 million at today's price of $400 an ounce. As the economy recovered and money became available again, gold mining increased once more, reaching its next peak in 1849 at 42,901 ounces. This was the period when the great lode mines reached their zenith. Mines sprung up with names like King Solomon's Mine, the Queen of Sheba, and the Black Cat. Towns with names like Gold Hill, in North Carolina, and Goldville, in Alabama, sprung up around the mines.

Gold Hill was probably the most famous mining area, and its output was prodigal. The area was first surveyed around 1823, but no one got around to digging seriously for gold there until 1843. By 1848, the area had more than 15 active mines worked by 1,000 or more miners. One mine, the Randolph, produced over $1.6 million in gold over its 100-year history.

As with most mining operations in the area, Gold Hill began with panning and placer operations. The farmers in Gold Hill, however, quickly latched on to the idea of sinking shafts to get the gold under the ground, and within the decade, they had discovered some nine veins within a 10-mile radius. These veins, moreover, were unusually rich and straight.

The miners at Gold Hill were also blessed with two other factors: relatively good local capital and an influx of Cornish immigrants, who brought with them knowledge of mining from their native land. As a result, the owners made good profits—in one case, about 1,000 percent—and relatively fewer miners were blown up, crippled, or buried alive at Gold Hill than elsewhere.

The work at Gold Hill was dark and dangerous, often at levels of 200 or more feet below the ground. To get the gold, miners had to blast out large sections of rock, haul it up, crush it, smelt it, and, ultimately, deliver it to the mint at Charlottesville. To get to the workings, miners had to climb down vertical ladders, often muddy and slippery, to the horizontal galleries. Light was provided by a single candle stuck to their hats with soft clay, and the pits were filled with the shouting of laborers, the booming of explosions, and the crashing of rock. To get out, they could climb back up the ladder, or, if in a hurry, jump on top of the horse-powered winches, or whims, that were used to haul up buckets of ore. The whims were quick, but dangerous, illustrating the dangers of doing anything on a whim.

Gold Hill outlived most of the other Southern gold mining areas, staying highly profitable until the onset of the Civil War. Other Southern gold mining areas took a bow far earlier. In 1848, when gold was discovered at Sutter's Mill, many of the Southern miners left wholesale, lured by the promise of easier gold. In an effort to keep the miners at Dahlonega, one Dr. Matthew Stephenson, an assayer at the mint, made an impassioned speech to the entire town. Pointing to the mountains, Stephenson cried, "There's gold in those hills! There's millions in it!"

The miners, who headed west shortly after Stephenson's speech, were struck by the phrase, and it became a rallying cry of the great Western gold rush. In *The Gilded Age,* Mark Twain immortalized it as "There's gold in them thar hills! There's millions in it!"

As the miners fled west, the Southern mines lapsed into decay. Mining engineer William Blake, writing in 1859, said:

> From 1849 to 1859, but little was done in the Georgia mines. . . . The mass of the people [in north Georgia] have neglected agriculture, especially those who, even for a time only, have lived by mining. The population has always been shifting, and many now prefer mining to any other employment. These dig about in the old diggings, and with a long tom, pick and spade, make a living for themselves and families, content, in general, if they realize enough to sustain life. The dissipation of former days have not wholly died out; many men who yet rely on their work in the mines for their subsistence, barter all their gold for whiskey, tobacco, meal and bacon. The gold may not be sufficient to obtain the needed quantities of all, but the gallon of whiskey must be had; the deficiency falls to meal and bacon.

Blake, who surveyed the mines in the area, thought there could be good money in reopening some of them, many of which had been worked down to the water level and then abandoned, as the miners often lacked proper pumping equipment. The miners also missed a lot of gold: At one site, he noted, many of the poor and the blacks supplemented what little income they had by panning for gold in the old tailings. He also thought that a new gold mining process, called the hydraulic method, which involved hosing down hillsides and capturing the sludge within them, could be used profitably. He was right on all counts, but the Civil War killed any plans of reopening the mines.

By the onset of the war, gold production all but ceased in the South. The Gold Hill mines, which had been highly profitable all through the 1850s, enjoyed a quick boom toward the end of the 1850s. A traveling business advisor in the mid-1850s noted that as long as several companies in Gold Hill competed with one another, Gold Hill production would be ineffient. The locals took his advice, joined forces, and went bankrupt in 1861. As the war escalated, lead became an infinitely more valuable commodity and was traded freely there until 1865. In fact, because lead was often found near the gold deposits, some Southern bullets had an unusually high gold content.

After the war, some of the miners drifted back, bringing with them the latest mining techniques from the West. They also brought back with them one of the easiest ways of making money from a gold mine: the stock certificate.

Twain once defined a gold mine as a hole in the ground with a liar standing in front of it. Although many of the more famous mines, such as the Barringer mine in North Carolina, reopened to booming success, the Southeastern mines quickly became tainted by fraud. The most common technique was to slap a fresh coat of paint on some old outbuildings, pump out the shafts, and bring in anxious investors.

If you had some cash to spend, you could "salt" the mines. The best way of doing this was to empty some shotgun shells of their birdshot, fill the shells with gold dust, and blast a few shots at the old mine walls. The gold dust would become convincingly spread about the walls, or at least enough so to get investors excited. Then you'd print up some certificates, sell them, and light out for the territories.

In any event, even the legitimate mines found the going increasingly tough. The mines reached their last great stage of production in the 1880s, at which point production fell off sharply. By the First World War, most of them had closed entirely.

The last gasp of the Southern mines was during the Great Depression, when gold prospecting, if not entirely profitable, was more interesting than staying at home. Once again some of the old mines were opened, and once again the prospective miners discovered that you have to pour a great deal of money into a mine before you get any out.

In Virginia, for example, gold was discovered just above the Cabin John Bridge, which spans the Potomac River and connects the town of Potomac with Washington, D.C. The gold in the Potomac valley had been discovered by members of a division of the union army called the 1st California. It was actually the 71st Pennsylvania, but they called themselves the 1st California in honor of their commander, Col. Edward Baker, who hailed from the Golden State. It's no wonder it took the Union four years to cross the 100 miles to Richmond.

At any rate, the regiment was camped out near Great Falls, Maryland, when some of the soldiers found gold. Two of the men returned and, with two others, formed the Maryland Mining Company. Another group, the Union Arch Gold Mining Company, had raised $2 million to start mines near the Cabin John Bridge.

As is often the case, the mines petered out quickly but speculation didn't. One William Kirk, for instance, sold interests in 10 gold mines in Fairfax County, promptly selling out his interests in the mines shortly after the new issue was completely subscribed. Kirk, among other things, enjoyed attending funerals to meet people. Eventually, Kirk himself succumbed to the allure of gold and mounted a serious effort at starting a mine in 1892. The venture collapsed four years later.

In the 1920s, his grandson made a stab at mining with the Virginia Gold Mining and Milling Company. They revived an old mine and, with much fanfare, reopened it in 1922. They then sold the property a year later. Some 11 years later, Kirk purchased yet another old gold mine on the Potomac and even managed to line up federal financing. In the darkest years of the Depression, the mine actually turned out a fair amount of gold. By 1940, however, the mine went under, never to reopen again.

Similar tales of reopened mines abounded throughout the Depression, although only a few managed to survive hard times. Today, you can count the serious gold mining operations in the South on one hand, even if you're missing a few fingers. All that's left of the great gold rush in the South are some shallow depressions, a few water-filled holes, and rusting outbuildings.

NEWMAN'S MINES

George Walter Newman's name is inexticably linked with the Gold Hill district of North Carolina. If anyone can think of a way to undo this, the citizens of Gold Hill will probably be happy to talk to you.[1]

Newman arrived shortly after his brother, Joe, and at about the same time as Thomas Alva Edison. Joe had come to scout out the gold mines in the area. Edison had come to figure out a better way of separating gold ore.[2]

Joe was impressed with the mining operations in Gold Hill and quietly bought a share in the mines. George came shortly thereafter, just in time for Joe's funeral. He died very, very suddenly.[3]

Newman now found himself the owner of an interest in a gold mine, which he quickly dubbed The Gold Hill Consolidated Company. The company's offices were on Broad Street in New York, and marks one of the earliest—and

---

[1]Overjoyed, in fact.
[2]It didn't work.
[3]His heart gave out when a load of dynamite exploded under his bed.

most successful—efforts to mine gold in the heart of the financial district in New York.

George quickly busied himself digging for gold among New Yorkers. He'd bring down potential investors by the trainload to inspect the mines at Gold Hill. They were almost invariably impressed.[4]

Newman built a mansion for himself on Gold Hill and treated his wife regally. He had a carriage built for her, complete with a sturdy, good-looking driver. He had some of the local boys to run ahead of the carriage and clear the path of any rocks that might cause her any discomfort.[5] Mrs. Newman's carriage must have been a thing of beauty, since one day she and her driver went for a ride and never came back.[6]

Newman was an unpredictable fellow, given to fits of generosity. These generally followed threats to dynamite someone's house.[7]

Life was hard after his wife died. His shareholders kept complaining, for example, that the stock never paid the dividends that had been promised. The stock never paid any dividends at all, in fact.[8]

Unfortunately, Newman wasn't a very good miner. According to one estimate, less than 1 percent of the gold mined was actually recovered. Finally, beset by increasing losses, Newman closed down the mines.

---

[4]Strewing gold nuggets on the floor of the mine almost always did the trick.
[5]Whether he paid them is doubtful.
[6]George was always too busy strewing nuggets around the mines.
[7]After Joe died, he didn't understand why people were always diving to the ground at loud noises.
[8]Some people just love to complain. He wrote to one disgruntled shareholder, "You are not worth the time it takes to insult you."

Just before World War I broke out, however, Newman made his final contribution to North Carolina gold mining history. He brought down another trainload of investors to view the mines, where a group of men were busily repairing the outbuildings.[9]

As they entered the mine—strewn with freshly bought gold nuggets—they saw the miners busily at work. These men were the same dozen or so men who, just a few minutes before, had been fixing up the outbuildings above.[10]

The investors were impressed—enough so to give Newman $12,000. The investors left and so did Newman. He left for New York and never returned to Gold Hill.

AFTERWORD

The story of North Carolina gold has remained largely untold, primarily because the great California gold rush eclipsed it so completely. In 1848, James Wilson Marshall discovered gold at Sutter's sawmill; by the next year, the first of some 100,000 goldminers were on their way to California. In five years, the California mines produced over 20 times the total production of the entire country.

Partly because California gold received so much attention, and partly because many important historical records were lost during the Civil War, many of the important historical details of the early Southern gold mines have been lost. Current scholarship into the mining communities of the South shows that the miners were, by and large, treated

---

[9]He made them pay their own way down, for once.
[10]Above all else, Newman valued hard work.

well by the standards of the day—which is to say, absolutely miserably by our standards.

The North Carolina gold rush is in this book primarily because it's one of the least-known—and the earliest—money manias in the country. And despite the fact that the gold fields in the South, the West, and Alaska have been largely played out, gold fever has never really died in this country. Instead, it remains endemic, lying dormant until the price of gold or the eruption of world uncertainty reignites it among otherwise sensible people.

It should be noted, incidentally, that there's a fundamental difference between someone who invests in gold and someone who rushes out to find gold. Buying gold, in general, is making a bet against civilization, or at least the established order of things. Gold, after all, has its greatest allure when the current scene is so frightening that one wants to hedge against the collapse of government-issued currency. For example, in order to finance the Civil War, the North issued greenbacks—currency that had no backing in gold. Then, as now, a dollar was worth whatever you thought it was. Naturally, whenever confidence in the dollar was high, it took fewer greenbacks to buy an ounce of gold. When things looked grim for the Union, the value of greenbacks fell.

Traders quickly took notice of this, and began posting agents around the battlefields. Word of a Union defeat would drive up the value of gold, and news of victory for the Union would drive down the value of gold. Because one could make a killing (as it were) on advance news of a battle, the people in the gold market often knew the outcome of a battle before Lincoln did. One can only imagine the sort of person who could survey the carnage of Anteitam, Shiloh, or Gettysburg and think first of trading.

Those who seek gold, on the other hand, are essentially optimists, although their optimism is rarely well-founded. The men and women who threw down their daily work to pan the streams of the Piedmont, for example, hoped to strike it rich, give up mining, and enjoy the finer things in life. Most of those who later went out west planned to stay a year, pull out a million or so in gold, and head back east. The bulk of them—those who lived, that is—settled in the West, and their fortunes eluded them. The country is richer for them, nevertheless.

While the California mining camps had the talents of a Mark Twain and a Bret Harte to chronicle the daily life and local color, there were no great recorders of what went on in the Southern gold fields. We know from contemporary accounts—particularly from Porte Crayon, the pseudononymous artist and reporter for *Harper's*—that the daily work at the mines was noisy and dangerous, and that those who dug the gold rarely, if ever, became rich. The same could be said for gold mines anywhere in the world today. We may never know much about the customs of the mining camps, or of those who came to the South to seek their fortunes in the gold fields.

If you page through an index of American historical writings over the years, you'll see 50 articles on California gold mines and mining to every one on the industry in the South. The most accessible sources of information about the southern gold rush comes from local historical societies and southern historians, who have taken the long, patient hours to comb through land records, short-lived local papers, and family genealogies to reconstruct something of boom. Two interesting books on the southern gold rush are Lou Harshaw's *The Gold of Dahlonega* and Bruce Roberts's *The Carolina Gold Rush*. Virginians will find *Fairfax Gold Fever,* by Walter Goetz, of particular interest.

Some of the most interesting recent work on the southern mines has come to light from the southern historical journals, particularly the work of Brent Glass in the *North Carolina Historical Review*. His careful analysis of the records at Gold Hill have produced a fine picture of life in one of the most famous of the southern boom towns. The explication of Nathaniel Hawthorne's allusion to Southern gold is the result of Margaret Moore's work in the *Essex Institute Historical Collections*.

SELECTED BIBLIOGRAPHY

Harshaw, Lou. *The Gold of Dahlonega*. Asheville, N.C.: Hexagon Co., 1976. One of the best explorations of the Georgia gold rush, profusely illustrated.

Nitze, Henry Benjamin Charles. *Gold Mining in North Carolina and Adjacent South Appalachian Regions*. Raleigh, N.C.: G. V. Barnes, 1897. One of the earliest surveys of the gold fields of the South.

Roberts, Bruce. *The Carolina Gold Rush*. Charlotte, N.C.: McNally and Loftin, 1971. One of the best sources of information on the southern gold rush.

Goetz, Walter. *Fairfax Gold Fever*. Privately published, 1968. Goetz managed to uncover mines that had been forgotten for over a hundred years.

CHAPTER 2

WASTE LAND

In a small room, a ritual takes place. Questions are asked. Oaths are taken. Covenants are made. Papers are signed, and seals are affixed on them. It's not an induction to the Great Order of Three-Eyed Wotan. It's the closing on a mortgage.

The similarity is not accidental. The word *mortgage* comes from an old French word for "death pledge." The term came about back in the Goode Olde Days, before herpes and real estate agents ruined everyone's fun. The death referred to, however, was not to the purchaser, but to the deal itself: If the buyer welshed on the payments, the deal was dead, and the property returned to the seller—or the lender, which was the more likely case.

To this day, real estate has one foot firmly in the Middle Ages. Real estate law is one of the oldest branches of Common Law, and its ground rules were set by people who felt it was perfectly all right to fillet your neighbor so long as you paid the survivors the proper number of chickens. Buying or selling a property is one of the most cumbersome processes on earth, involving bankers, lawyers, and agents. What's worse, you have to rely on a string of buyers and sellers across the country in order to close your deal—which means that if some jerk in Tulsa had a lien slapped on his house because he didn't pay off the aluminum siding, the entire deal could collapse.

You'd think that such a wearisome process would be the last place in which speculation would flourish. You'd be wrong.

Americans, who have been blessed with so much empty land, have a reverence for real estate that borders on fanaticism. Although the desire to find gold was a driving motive behind the early exploration of the country, the desire to own land was no less a force. The upshot has been our tendency to make our single largest investment with the help of someone who is paid to look after the other party's interest.

The history of real estate in this country has been checkered with booms and busts. It may surprise you, however, to know that the biggest real estate boom was not in the 1980s, but in the 1830s—a time when much land was free, at least for those who didn't mind clearing it with their bare hands. And when the boom went bust in 1837, it caused the biggest depression in the nation's history, at least until the time when Wall Street laid an egg in October 1929.

Manias always have a good story behind them, and the optimism of the 1830s was certainly well-founded. The wars with Britain were over; the country stretched from the East Coast to the Rockies, and much of it was unsettled and barely explored. Farmland was being cleared at an astounding rate. Technology was booming: Steam was being harnessed for power, and the new power was revolutionizing travel and transport by means of steamships and railroads.

At first blush, it would seem that nothing could go wrong, particularly given the country's abundance at the time. Of course, this is the way it always seems whenever something really terrible happens. And things started to go wrong right from the start.

Just how everything went wrong is a complicated story. In fact, just what prompts entire countries to give themselves up to speculation—and the inevitable depressing aftermath—is in itself a matter of intense speculation. Some people think it's a naturally recurring phenomenon, like lemmings hurling themselves into the sea or Red Sox fans telling themselves that the Old Towne Team really can win the pennant. People who follow this school of thought think that all things economic, like things astronomical, run in cycles. Just as Neptune whirls around the earth every 250 years or so, so do really bad financial events occur in predictable cycles. Cyclists of the financial sort spend an awful lot of time looking for patterns, subpatterns and subsubpatterns that continue to occur throughout history.

Those who believe in cycles—the stock market technician, Robert Prechter, is perhaps the chief spokesman for the group today—are convincing, and often successful, at least for a while. But when their theories fall in on themselves, as Prechter's did in October 1987, they often seem like the arguments of the Ptolomaic astronomers, who believed the sun rotated around the earth. Things kept happening that they couldn't explain, so the Ptolomaic astronomers had to invent new subtheories to start to explain them. Prechter, whose Eliott Wave Theory said that the grand cycle of the stock market would peak at 3,600 on the Dow Jones industrial average, had to rethink his theories so that they would fit a Dow top at slightly over 2,700.

Others, economists mainly, think that manias and panics result from a combination of complex events, somewhat in the same way that hurricanes do. According to economic theory, manias—and the panics that inevitably follow—are precipitated by a shock or dislocation to the economic system. The Arab oil embargo is a classic example of a shock that precipitated, if not a panic, a major bear market in the real estate and stock markets from 1973 to 1975.

On the whole, the economists are probably right. Their only real problem is that the mechanisms of the economy—like the workings of weather—are too complex to allow any sort of accuracy in prediction. Economists, like weathermen, make predictions mainly because people expect them to.

In simpler terms, manias and panics happen whenever too many people think they've figured out how to get rich. Walter Bagehot, in his "Essay on Edward Gibbon," put his finger on it neatly:

> At particular times, a great deal of stupid people have a great deal of stupid money. . . . At intervals . . . the money of these people is particularly large and craving; it seeks for someone to devour it, and there is a "plethora"; it finds someone, and there is "speculation"; it is devoured, and there is "panic."

That quote, incidentally, is found in the beginning of *Manias, Panics and Crashes,* by Charles Poor Kindleberger, a book that remains one of the most authoritative works on the subject.

At any rate, the 1830s had one thing in common with nearly every boom time in history: It was preceded by a period of generally rising prices. In 1920, for example, the high cost of living was a general topic of conversation. Nine years later, in 1929, the stock market headed for oblivion. Inflation was the obsession of the country in 1980, with investors throwing their money into anything not backed by increasingly worthless paper: gold, jojoba beans, and the like. In 1987, the stock market took a dive that put 1929's Black Thursday to shame. And, if you care to delve into panics and depressions further, you'll find inflationary periods before the panics of 1857, 1866, 1873, 1894, and 1907 as well.

The inflation of the early 1830s had several causes. First of all, the population was growing, and, by and large, the population was employed. Although wages then were not huge—a worker in the mills of Lowell, Massachusetts, could look forward to making about $1 a day—they were certainly worth writing home about, particularly if your home was in Europe, where workers made about a third of that. So people had money to spend, and, as the population increased, demand for the basics, like coal and shoes, increased as well. As demand increases, so do prices, so long as there's only a limited amount of what's being sold. It's the way the world works.

A rising tide lifts all ships, and the biggest ship to float in the tide of inflation was cotton, the ruling crop of the South. Cotton prices rose steadily throughout the decade, and demand for it soared not only in the industrial North, but throughout the world as well. The rise in cotton prices had two effects: It gave the illusion that cotton prices had nowhere to go but up, and it made many Southern planters rich. Ultimately, of course, the illusion that cotton was king would lead, at least in part, to the Civil War.

In times of inflation, people figure out that something worth $1.00 today might be worth $1.50 next year, and start thinking about how to get in on the receiving end of that process. Of course, the people who are already getting the benefits of higher prices—people who own farms and factories, for example—are thinking along the same lines. What's more, they now have more money than they used to and are eager to put it to work.

Since times were flush, those who were the flushest started thinking in terms of dumping the old Colonial mansion for something a bit more flashy: Greek Revival was all the rage back then. "The Joneses have a lovely mansion with pillars; why shouldn't we?" was probably heard up and down the East Coast. And, as the wealthy began to buy, land prices began to rise.

The price increases began gradually in the 1830s, in the most logical places: the cities, where trade and commerce flourished, and where the most people with the most money lived. As real estate became pricier in the cities, such as New York, price rises spread outward to where people could afford a piece of the action. And in the unbridled optimism of the 1830s, everywhere was full of promise.

In New York City, which was already a heck of a town even though they drove pigs down the middle of the streets, the price of a lot rose steadily. In 1835, for example, most of the city burned down, which is what happens when you build too many frame houses too close together. When some of the burned-out lots went up for auction shortly thereafter, they commanded higher prices than they would have before the fire—with buildings on them. And the buildings that had burned really weren't that bad. By 1836, lots 25 feet by 100 fetched $12,000 in lower Manhattan. That may sound like a steal to you, particularly since rent in New York now starts at $200 a minute, but remember that a dollar then was worth several hundred times what it's worth now and that parts of Uptown—that is, below Harlem, which was a town in its own right—were still farmland.

True to form, price increases radiated out from New York. In Buffalo, prime land rose from $500 an acre to $10,000 an acre in 1836. Even given that Buffalo was, at the time, a relatively important town, those prices were astronomical. But Buffalo shared its good fortune with other towns that didn't have much promise then and don't have much now—towns like Dunkirk, Van Buren, and Black Rock. At Van Buren, a group of men bought 300 acres at $25 each, formed a company, and sold 75 shares of stock at $100. The shares ran up to $3,000 each, turning a $1,875 purchase into $225,000.

In the hinterlands of Maine, uninhabited land went from $5 to $15, while lots in Bangor went from $200 to $1,000. Prices in the South rose as well, with homes in Natchez fetching nearly as much as brownstones in New York, while the city of New Orleans grew flush with the cash from cotton.

And in the West, where the government was selling off its inventory of public lands, riots broke out at public land sales, as speculators crowded out immigrants longing to own land. Investors from the East and from abroad guessed, rightly, that the vast stretches of woods and prairies on the other side of the mountains wouldn't stay bucolic forever. Just as today's developers can look at a patch of farmland and envision parking lots, the speculators of the 1830s could look at vast tracts of woods and see farmlands, towns, and cities.

Another hallmark of a boom is the rise of con men and frauds, who can look at the madness about them and realize that some people will buy anything. And so it was in the 1830s, when some of these farms, towns, and cities were only in the eyes of the crooks. These men would map out entirely fictitious towns, complete with opera houses and town halls, and sell lots to unsuspecting Easterners. Towns like Port Sheldon, Michigan, and Kankakee City, Illinois, were largely lots marked off in a field, although the promoters of Port Sheldon did get around to building some roads, a lighthouse, and a hotel. Lots in Marion City, Missouri, which sold for $200 to $1,000, needed considerable improvement: They were under six feet of water.

Although speculation relied upon credulous investors, it was made easier by the banks, who would lend against the value of the land, thus allowing buyers to purchase great tracts with very little of their own money. This is the most sensible and profitable way to do so, provided property prices in general continue to go up. The reason has to do with what real estate agents tend to call "the magic of leverage." Suppose you buy a $10,000 piece of property with $1,000 of your own money and $9,000 borrowed from the bank. If you sell two years later for $12,000, you still have to pay the bank $9,000, but you get to pocket the additional $2,000 and keep your original $1,000. Not counting your borrowing costs, you've tripled your money, even though your investment rose only 20 percent.

Real estate agents tend to talk about "the joys of home ownership" when the magic of leverage wears off. And it can wear off very quickly, as anyone in Texas or Massachusetts can tell you. The reason: When prices start going down, you'd better enjoy living in your home, because you won't have any money when you sell. Suppose your $10,000 house depreciated by 20 percent to $8,000 instead of appreciating to $12,000. You'd still owe your bank $9,000 because bankers are sticklers on points like that. So you would have lost your $1,000 investment and still owe another $1,000 on the deal—a 200 percent loss.

Nevertheless, borrowing to buy land isn't bad, particularly if you plan to stay where you are for the foreseeable future. Otherwise, most people couldn't afford to buy a home. When credit and speculation mix, however, the upshot is often disastrous. Naturally, this is exactly what happened.

The fact that banks could—and did—issue currency didn't help. The peculiar rules that govern banks dictate that a debt owed to a bank, such as a mortgage, is counted as an asset. The more assets you have, the more you can lend. So if you were an up-and-coming bank, the road to prosperity was paved with loans. From this mindset the worst problems grew. A bank could make a loan on a real estate purchase, for example, and then accept the property for collateral on yet another real estate loan, and so on, ad absurdum. The upshot was a string of mortgages on which very little money actually rested.

In the South, where the economy relied mainly on agriculture, banks proved even more obliging. A farmer could deposit his cotton crop with a local bank-approved storehouse, and receive the going price for cotton. To make life easier, the bank would issue the farmer credit for about 25 percent of his crop. Cotton, after all, was king, and it would never decline in value. Some banks even accepted slaves as collateral for loans.

To make matters worse, the banks then issued currency based on their assets. Then, as now, paper currency was simply a promise to pay by the issuer of the note. At the time, the federal government was out of the business of issuing paper currency. During the period of the Articles of Confederation, the script issued by the federal government depreciated so badly that it ultimately became almost worthless. The preferred method of payment was via the Spanish milled dollar, or rial—the legendary "piece of eight," so called because it was often chopped up into eighths, or bits. In case you're wondering, the rial was the only method of payment in the fledgling stock market in New York, and to this day stock prices are quoted in eighths.

At any rate, carrying around $5 or more in gold is cumbersome, so banks obliged by issuing currency. The best currency was issued by the Bank of the United States, but smaller banks got into the act as well, often issuing script in denominations of less than $5. Many banks would issue $15 in notes for every $1 in coin that they had in their vaults; others were even more liberal in printing notes because they had nothing behind their notes at all. Aside from being dubious banking practice, printing money fanned the inflationary fires: As you pump more cash into the system, people think less of paying more for goods and services.

The one force standing in the way of all this madness was the Bank of the United States. It was, at that time, the most powerful institution in the country, and one fifth of it was owned by the U.S. government. Its purpose was to take deposits, issue currency, and lend money in the money market.

The Bank of the United States was run by the most formidable banker until Paul Volcker, the Chairman of the Federal Reserve Bank under Presidents Carter and Reagan. His name was Nicholas Biddle. Biddle started out as a member of the American legation to France, which settled some of the spoils of the Napoleonic war. After dabbling in literature for a while, he served a term in the Pennsylvania House of Representatives and then landed a job as director of the Bank of the United States. He became its president in 1822 and managed to stabilize the currency issued by the bank, primarily by stabilizing the bank itself.

As head of the chief bank, Biddle wielded enormous power, but it wasn't a popular post. One Federal Reserve banker defined a central bank's job as "taking away the punch bowl once the party gets going." In 1833, Biddle, worried about the creeping manias in the money markets, decided to do something about it. Biddle started to clear the table by making loans harder to get and calling in others for payment. The predictable result was a slowdown in business across the country, business failures, and layoffs.

By cooling off the economy—and particularly the smaller banks—Biddle hoped to cool off inflation as well. With money harder to get, people would be less willing to pay higher prices for things. Biddle did cool down the economy but also earned himself even more enmity from General Andrew Jackson who, unfortunately for Biddle, also happened to be president at the time. Jackson, for numerous reasons besides the slowdown of 1833 to 1834, opposed the renewal of the bank's charter in 1836. While Old Hickory's actions didn't cause the ensuing panic, it certainly didn't help it.

Biddle eased up on the reins in 1834, and the country rallied into 1835 and 1836. The land sales continued, and money kept pouring into government coffers. By 1836, the government had no debt whatsoever. You couldn't buy a Treasury bond for love nor money. In fact, the government was sitting on a surplus of $37 million by the opening days of 1837.

The states, however, more than made up for the federal government's thrift. The reason was simple. Good farmland on the East Plunkett River is all well and good, but if the farmers can't deliver their beans to market, it really doesn't make any sense to open up the land. You might as well sell it back to the French. So the states rushed into improving their territories with a vengeance.

Building roads was the states' first foray into land improvements, but roads have limitations, particularly when you haven't invented the semitrailer yet. There's only so much you can load onto a horse or several horses. If you want to move a great deal of goods, such as cotton, wheat, or corn, you need something with a bit more carrying power. Something like a canal, for instance.

Canals were wildly popular in the early 1800s and for good reason: It's a lot easier to drag goods over water than it is over land. Easier on the horses, too. Massachusetts was the first state to start building canals, with the Middlesex canal connecting Lowell to the seaports on the coast. Other states quickly followed: The Erie Canal linked upstate New York with the Great Lakes and, ultimately, Chicago via the Hudson River. The canal had been planned as early as

1783, but finding financing took another 34 years. Individual investors wouldn't take the risk; neither would the federal government. Finally De Witt Clinton ran for governor of New York, with the building of the canal as his sole platform. He won, and the waterway was opened in 1825 at a cost of over $7 million, much of it borne by his new constituents.

The canal was a rousing success, and New Yorkers figured that if one canal was good, then a dozen or so would be just grand. As a result, the state also built the Oswego, the Cayuga and Seneca, the Chenango, the Crooked Lake, and the Chemung canals. By 1840, New York had some 736 miles of canals, at a cost of $12 million. None of the canals were as successful as the Erie Canal. As you may have noticed, no one ever wrote any songs about working 16 years on the Chemung Canal.

New York's success led other states into the canal mania. Pennsylvania had 700 miles of canals by 1831, for example, and Maryland and Virginia each boasted ambitious canal projects. Ohio spent about $8 million on a variety of works, including four canals.

One of the more ambitious copiers of the Erie canal was the Morrison Canal, originally planned to link the Hudson River with Newark and, eventually, Jersey City. The company was planned as both a canal and banking company, which was one of the more novel permutations of the canal business at the time. The banking arm of the Morrison Canal and Banking Company was to be used to finance yet more canals. The company sold 20,000 shares of stock at $100 per share in 1825 and opened the first leg of the canal in 1832.

Even as most of the canals were being built, however, they were becoming obsolete. In 1827, just across the state from the first canal in Lowell, Massachusetts, the people of

Quincy completed the first railroad. Although just a short line for hauling granite from its quarries, the new railroad would sound the death knell for the Middlesex Canal—as well as for all those built during the great period of internal improvements. The days of canal boats in America would be brief.

The planners in the states realized the importance of the railroads and made plans for them as well, although many of the railroads were private enterprises. That didn't stop the builders of the railroads from issuing bonds to pay for them, or the states from offering support. Even as the first leg of the Chesapeake and Ohio Canal was being opened in Maryland, Charles Carroll of Carrolton, the state's only surviving signer of the Declaration of Independence, was officiating at the start of the Baltimore and Ohio Railroad. The line was to run from Baltimore to Ohio, and the state subscribed to both ventures to the tune of $12 million.

Foreign investors were also intrigued by the possibilities of America and poured cash into the country for a variety of ventures. Some of these ventures actually had a chance of succeeding, while others were simply yet another way for smart Americans to fleece unsuspecting investors.

By 1836, the bubble was ripe for bursting. Guy Salisbury, a historian in Buffalo, described the mood in that halcyon year:

> It is touching, almost, to dwell upon the generous, trusting confidence which the speculators of '36 manifested. Nothing was to impossible for them to believe in, or to promise. . . . They prophesied, those speculators, like the inspired Pythoness, of the Future, and casting aside the things that were behind, pressed forward for those which were before. . . . They built, on paper, the splendid Perry Monument, of white American marble, one hundred feet high (which you can't see), in front of the Churches. They in like visionary manner, erected the noble college edifice on North Street, for the

University of Western New York, which was so magnifi-
cently endowed (by subscription) with professorships that
rivaled the princely largesses of the Lawrences and the Ap-
pletons. They gazed with pride and satisfaction upon the
massive foundations which Rathbun had commenced of that
stupendous Exchange, whose lofty dome was to tower two
hundred and twenty feet above the pavement on the Clar-
endon Square!

Needless to say, none of the above noble edifices were ever
built. But so it went across the country. Land prices kept
rising, even as the government sold off more and more of
the public lands. In 1833, the government had peddled $4.2
million worth of public lands; it sold slightly under that in
the second quarter of 1835. Land sales totaled $24.9 million
in 1836.

As the land sales grew, so did the abuses. Charges of
fraud in the land offices were frequent and, in many cases,
absolutely true. Maps of public lands to be sold were often
leaked out early, so that speculators could get the best
tracts. In some offices, obliging cartographers would mark
some lands as already sold before they went to market.

Just as bubbles have many causes, the end of bubbles
also have many causes. One of the prime culprits in the
bursting of the 1836 bubble was the Specie Circular. In
banking terms, specie is cold, hard cash, and it was Jackson's favorite form of currency. He detested banks, and
thought that paper money was at the root of any number of
evils, among them the land fever. So he formulated the
Specie Circular as a way to squash speculation. In essence,
the Circular said that after August 15, 1836, you had to pay
for land in specie. The one exception was made for bona fide
settlers, who could pay with bank notes until December 15.

The move squashed land speculation, all right, but it
did more than that. Since you had to pay for land with cash,
those buying land or moving west took specie with them out

west—which resulted in a fairly rapid loss of cash in the East. Since the cash went from the speculators in the West back into the government's coffers, money quickly became tight all over.

The Bank of the United States could probably have helped the situation by lending out more cash, but it had unfortunately ceased to exist by 1837. Jackson decided not to renew its charter, and Biddle knew he was overpowered. He finally managed to get a state charter for the bank in Pennsylvania, but the bank's ability to influence events was greatly diminished.

The one ray of hope in the situation was the government surplus, which could have pumped some $37 million in desperately needed cash into the system. And, in fact, the government planned to distribute the surplus in 1837 back to the states in four equal installments.

Unfortunately, the distribution of the surplus depended on the banks to distribute it, and they weren't up to the task. The Treasury, at that point, consisted of accounts in deposit banks in each of the states. Forcing these banks to make large cash payments at a time when cash was growing short was disastrous. Quite simply, the move forced the biggest and strongest lenders to pull in their horns in order to make the distributions—which meant they had to either stop making loans or to call in the loans that they had made. The overall effect was like stepping on the air hose of a dying patient. Three distributions were made in 1837; by the time the fourth distribution came due, there simply wasn't any left. For the first—and only—time in history, the United States defaulted on its obligations.

By the fall of 1837, events quickly turned for the worse. Inflation was still rampant, and, by February, rioting broke out in New York City over the price of food. Mobs gathered at storefronts and looted kegs of flour, a typically stupid mob action that ruined both the flour and the store owner at the same time.

At the same time, the credit markets began realizing that cash was hard to get. Interest rates, which ran at 5 to 6 percent annually during the balmier days of 1836, ran up to 24 percent in short order. Banks, desperate for cash, stopped making loans entirely and called in whatever loans were owed. Here the banks' looseness with credit turned on them, as it quickly became apparent that many of the loans were absolutely worthless. The weaker banks began to announce that they could no longer pay $10 in cash for $10 notes they had issued. Some refused to honor their notes at all. This was bad enough in and of itself, but it also had another effect: People began to horde cash as bank notes became increasingly worthless. The bad money drove out the good.

The rest of the country then went broke. In March of 1837, a large cotton broker went bankrupt, causing the collapse of J. L. & S. Joseph & Company, a large dry-goods dealer. By April, hundreds of businesses, ranging from stockbrokers to banks to grocers, went under. Among the April casualties, were 28 real estate speculators, with $28 million in capital, and 8 stockbrokers, with $1 million in capital.

Land prices, of course, also rode off into the sunset. Buffalo, which aimed to be the Athens of the North, saw prices crash to about one-twentieth of their values in the torrid days of 1836. Lots that sold for $35 a foot quickly sank to $2 a foot. In New York, prices tumbled by a third or more. And in the shiningly planned communities in the West, prices sank to almost nothing. The grand hotel in Port Sheldon, Michigan, for example, was carted away for the cost of scrap, and cows still graze contentedly on the site of Kankakee City.

As if things weren't bad enough, money became tight in England as well, effectively turning off the spigot from abroad. At the height of the boom, foreign money, particularly from England, was a gusher. The English bought the American dream as well, and in 1837, they found themselves much the poorer for it. Up to a quarter of the issues traded in London were American-based, and in the heady times before the crash, English investors couldn't get enough of them. After the crash, many became worthless. One estimate puts the English losses in 1837 at about $130 billion.

Money soon became tighter than a pawnbroker's smile, and a group of states looking to sell bonds were turned away from both London and New York. The great rush to improving the national landscape came to a screeching halt, and thousands were thrown out of work. As money became scarce, prices went down, and the country fell into a depression that would take it seven long years to pull out from under.

Banks didn't resume payment on their notes for a full year, during which time the country operated on a peculiar barter system, exchanging near-worthless bank notes at elaborate discount rates or exchanging goods and services outright. A trip from Vermont to Richmond, for example, involved trading bank notes at nearly every stop along the way and generally losing money each time. In these types of exchanges, proximity was a major factor in trading: A note from a bank in Vermont became progressively more worthless the further you traveled from the bank's doors.

A popular joke of the time involved a visitor at one of New York's theaters. On the curtain were the letters S.P.Q.R.—the emblem of the Roman Republic. The visitor asked a friend what the letters stood for. His reply: "Specie Payments Quite Rare." It was considered a real rip-snorter in its day, although it might have lost some of its luster over the decades.

It was a bad time to be any sort of investor. Even as land prices plummeted and bond issuers defaulted, the stock market crashed as well. Hardest hit were the canal and railway shares. Morrison Canal, which had become a speculative favorite during the boom years, fell from a little over $100 in January 1837 to less than $50 per share in April. The company never really recovered and disappeared in 1844. Harlem Railroad, which sold for $83 a share in January 1837, sold for $52 a share in April of that year.

Banking shares fared little better, although the Bank of the United States fared the least poorly, dropping from $116 per share in January to about $100 per share in April. Farmers Loan & Trust fell about 20 percent from its January highs. The fall in 1837, however, was just the beginning, and anyone who owned bank stocks probably ceased to believe in them as a long-term investment. Farmers' Trust stock eventually bottomed out at about $30 per share, while the Bank of the United States' stock swooned to $4 per share.

It wasn't until the late 1840s before the country entered its next boom period. Martin Van Buren, who rode in on Andrew Jackson's coattails, lost his bid for reelection. Nicholas Biddle ventured on speculation in the cotton market and lost a fortune for himself and his friends. By the end of the decade, however, the discovery of gold in California, as well as a rising interest in American railroads by foreigners, ushered in a new period of rising prices and speculation. The upshot was, of course, the panic and depression of 1857. After that came the Civil War.

GEORGE WASHINGTON, LAND BARON

Even though George Washington was a national figure, his heart was always back home in Virginia.[1]

Washington's love affair with Virginia[2] probably started when he was a young surveyor. As he crisscrossed the commonwealth, he noticed its wild splendor, its vast forests, its huge tracts of land going for next to nothing. He resolved to buy as much of it as possible.[3] His resolution led him to be one of the best-known real estate speculators in America and a canal-builder, as well.

Washington worked hard, became a soldier in the King's army, and married rich. Soon thereafter, he also became a major landowner.[4]

During the dark days of the Revolution, Washington thought often of Virginia. He thought particularly of the

---

[1]Martha may have been another story.
[2]The state, that is.
[3]He bought his first lot at 18.
[4]People look down at marrying money. Washington certainly did all right.

huge tracts of land he'd bought that were virtually impossible to get to.[5]

Much of the land Washington owned had choice river frontage on the Potomac or its tributaries. At Mount Vernon, which is just a few miles below what is now Washington, D.C., the Potomac flows slowly and majestically to the Chesapeake Bay.[6]

A few miles upriver, however, the Potomac enters an area called Little Falls. Just up the river is Great Falls.[7] The river has a few placid stretches further on, but the average boat would be smashed to flinders on parts of the upper Potomac.[8]

Washington first tried advertising as a way to smooth over the problems with his land holdings. For example, he advertised a holding he had with his partner, one William Crawford. The land, some 30,000 acres of it, was on the Virginia side of the Ohio River.[9] "The So. East side of the Ohio can give no jealousy to the Indians . . . the proprietors may cultivate their Farms in peace, and fish, and fowl and hunt without fear of molestation."

Crawford, unfortunately, died shortly thereafter. He was tortured and burned at the stake by the Indians near Upper Sandusky, Ohio.[10]

Washington soon became convinced that opening the Potomac to trade would be a great national feat and pushed

---

[5]It's no fun owning land if you have to hike two weeks to get there.
[6]It's too broad to throw a silver dollar across, though.
[7]Strangely enough, there's a great falls there.
[8]That takes away a lot of the advantage of owning riverfront property.
[9]West Virginia wouldn't be along for another 90 years or so.
[10]Washington, for his part, was "excited to tears."

it as a way to keep the Western settlers in touch with the rest of the country. To do so, he proposed a series of canals that would circumvent the worst patches of the Potomac.

To that end, Washington formed the Potowmack Company, whose ambition was to open the river clear to Cumberland, some 185 miles northwest of Washington. The company was formed in 1785, and George bought five shares at 100 pounds a share. The state of Virginia kicked in 50 shares.[11]

The company was chartered in Virginia, which was a problem since Maryland owned the river. Washington quickly gathered all parties together at Mount Vernon to discuss the issue and got both states to agree to compromise.[12] Maryland and Virginia ratified the agreement, which was illegal under the Articles of Confederation.[13]

This situation didn't last long, however, since the Constitutional Convention convened soon afterward, making it easier for states to make agreements between each other, among other things.

Work began on the canal almost at once, and its shareholders immediately became poorer.[14] Construction of the canal—which entailed five canals around difficult points and several dredging operations as well—lasted until 1802, two years after Washington's death.

---

[11]The fact that Washington was president of the company probably had nothing to do with Virginia's contribution.

[12]See footnote 11.

[13]Washington made exceptions from time to time, such as his purchases of land in areas where it was forbidden to purchase land.

[14]It was a joint-stock company, which allows shareholders to enjoy the company's losses as well as its profits.

The main problem was getting around Great Falls, which entails a 77-foot drop. Washington, at first, didn't want to use locks, which were expensive. His engineers had to explain that the drop, even if it were in the form of a water chute, would kill most people who went down it.

Workers were hard to get, and wages included whiskey to keep them happy. That caused other problems, however—particularly among those who handled the black powder for blasting: They often went to pieces.[15]

Once the canal was completed, it spent another 26 years going bankrupt. For a while, a thriving town called Matildaville grew up near the Great Falls locks.[16] Matildaville wasn't destined for greatness either, and the last surviving building there, a tavern, called it quits in 1923.

The canal had several problems. It was narrow, for one thing, and only certain types of boats could pass. In many cases, these were the wrong types of boats. For another, there were only a few weeks a year when the river was high enough to allow a boat with a one-foot draft to navigate the entire way, and periodic floods of the Potomac tended to make passage impossible.

The canal was bought in 1828 by the C&O Canal across the river, which took another 100 years to go bankrupt. Nowadays you can see the remains of Washington's canal on the Virginia side of Great Falls.

---

[15]"We have been very much imposed upon in the last two weeks in the powder way," the Potowmack's engineer wrote. "We had our blowers, one run off the other blown up."

[16]Washington owned land there, too.

AFTERWORD

The panic of 1837 was not the country's first panic, nor was it the first general downturn in business conditions. The United States started out on shaky financial footing even before it was born, and one of the most fertile grounds for genealogical explorations among those determined to find a patriot in the family tree are the numerous petitions to Congress for long-overdue Revolutionary War pensions. During the time of the Articles of Confederation, U.S. currency became utterly worthless, a situation that helped speed the movement toward the strong central government promulgated by the Constitution.

The country had at least one other major period of panic and depression before 1837, a short, sharp downturn from 1818 to 1819. After the 1837 debacle, panics occurred with depressing regularity—in 1857, 1873, 1893, and 1907, to name just the major ones. Of the 19th-century panics, however, the crisis of 1837 remains the major one, with only the 1857 panic coming close to it in duration or intensity. Of all depressions in U.S. history, only the Great Depression of 1929 to 1939 eclipses 1837.

Although much ink has been expended on the 1929 crash, the 1837 crash has received considerably less attention. The main reason, of course, is that the Great Depression was within living memory; those of us who did not live through it know someone who did, and the stories from that era are compelling. The events of the panic of 1837 are removed by several generations, and few stories have filtered down so far.

The story of the panic of 1837 is in this book for precisely that reason. Even though all unhappy events are different in many respects, they have a fair number of similarities as well. Anyone who lived through the 1920s will probably recognize the unbridled optimism and raw speculation that characterized the 1830s; anyone who lived through the 1930s will probably recognize the general business collapse that followed.

For those who long for the days of a limited government role in the economy, the crisis of 1836 should also provide little support. In 1836, there was no central bank or lender of last resort, with the possible exception of the Bank of England, to bail out the economy. The thought of government programs to aid those thrown out of work was, by and large, entirely an entirely alien notion in those days. Whether or not a strong central bank or the government could have bailed out the country is still a source of debate, but the decade that followed was known as "the hungry 40s"—primarily because business conditions were so bad. The saving factor in the late 1840s was the discovery of gold in California, which injected huge amounts of new cash into the economy.

Later 19th-century panics, incidentally, should add little fuel to those who advocate gold as the backbone of the nation's currency. There simply isn't much evidence to prove that gold does a much better job of backing currency than nothing at all. In fact, the major difference between gold-backed currency and pure paper seems to be that gold-backed currency tends to lead toward depressions and falling prices in hard times, while paper-backed currency leads to inflation and rising prices during hard times. What's more, since the government is often the single greatest buyer and seller of gold when the yellow metal backs the currency, it's relatively easy for the government to manipulate the economy through its own purchases and sales of gold.

Much of the work done on the panic of 1836 comes from economists and other academics. The why of the panic of

1837 is preserved, primarily, in such works as Charles Poor Kindleberger's *Manias, Panics, and Crashes,* and Robert Sobel's *Panic on Wall Street.* Peter Temin's *The Jacksonian Economy* provides tremendous detail on the speculation in land, canals, and railroads that preceded the crash. Contemporary accounts, in the forms of magazine articles and tracts, also help to fill in the picture.

SELECTED BIBLIOGRAPHY

Kindleberger, Charles Poor, *Manias, Panics, and Crashes: A History of Financial Crises.* New York: Basic Books, Inc., 1978. *The* book for anyone who wants to understand the basic mechanisms of financial crises.

Sobel, Robert, *Panic on Wall Street: A History of America's Financial Disasters.* New York: MacMillan, 1969. Sobel views the 1837 panic through the journal of a prosperous New Yorker, as well as through the banking statistics of the day. A fine book for anyone interested in any of the major U.S. fiscal crises.

Temin, Peter, *The Jacksonian Economy.* New York: Norton, 1969. A wonderfully readable and finely researched work on how the early U.S. financial system functioned—and misfunctioned.

CHAPTER 3

ERIE EVENTS ON WALL STREET

Wall Street has always had a fondness for nicknames. Jacob Little, for example, earned the name of "Ursa Major"—the great bear—in part by inventing the short sale, which makes it as easy to lose money when stocks rise as it is when they fall. Unlike many others, however, Little sold short successfully, most notably during the panic of 1837. As the stock market crashed and the country plunged into a seven-year depression, Little earned a fortune.

Little got quite a bit of practice at making fortunes, having made and lost four of them by 1857. His last words were, "I'm going up, boys! Who's going with me?" Whether he was referring to the market or the Choir Invisible is unclear, but he got no takers. In an uncharacteristic gesture, Wall Street gave him a grand funeral, probably because he'd enriched so many of his fellow speculators.

Despite his notoriety, Little was to go down in history as Ursa Minor, or the Little Bear. He was overshadowed by Daniel Drew, the greatest bear ever seen on the Street. Drew was also called Uncle Dan'l, the Speculative Director, and the Old Bear—in public. What his victims called him privately is probably best left to the imagination. Whatever Drew did, tales of his treachery, deceit and duplicity followed him. Most of them were probably true.

For example, Drew once wanted revenge on some fellow speculators who had made fun of him when he was in a tight spot in the market. One hot summer night, he appeared in a local tavern where his quarry would come to drink and spread rumors. Drew walked in, looked around anxiously, and mopped his brow. As he drew his handkerchief, a scrap of paper fell out of his pocket. One of the speculators put his foot over the paper.

When Drew walked out, the men crowded around to read the note. It was an order to Drew's broker. "Buy all the shares of Oshkosh you can get your hands on," said the note, in Drew's hand. The next day, the brokers pooled their cash and bought a large block of Oshkosh, hoping to catch the rise as Drew bought. Oshkosh dropped like a hang glider in an air pocket. And no wonder. The stock they bought was from Drew himself, who had sold enough to offset the speculator's purchases—and then some. Like many others before them, they had learned the hard way never to underestimate Daniel Drew.

Drew's greatest moment came in 1867, when the Speculative Director clashed head-on with none other than Cornelius Vanderbilt, whose $70 million fortune made him the second-richest man in the country (William Astor was the wealthiest.) Vanderbilt was called the "Commodore," partly from a minor role in the War of 1812 as an army supply-ship captain, and partly from the fact that he monopolized the steamboat business between New York City and Albany. Besides, Vanderbilt liked the ring of the title, and when you have that much money, people tend to call you what you like—to your face, at least. Out of earshot, they called him Old Seventy Millions.

Vanderbilt was not a man to be lightly crossed. When his wife refused to move from Staten Island to Manhattan, the Commodore had her committed to an insane asylum for two years. He banished his own son to an island farm for nearly 20 years. And when he learned that he'd been double-crossed by some business partners, he wrote, "The law takes too long—I'll ruin you." He did, too.

Arrogant, handsome, semiliterate, foul-tongued and bullheaded, Vanderbilt was to become the immovable rock to Drew's irresistible force. The Drew-Vanderbilt showdown was probably the greatest sting operation in Wall Street history.

The object of both men's fancy was the New York and Erie Railroad, one of the most compelling arguments against the efficiency of private enterprise. The line was envisioned as link between New York City and Buffalo, a railroad equivalent of the Erie Canal. It didn't make it to either city. The line's southern terminus was Piermont, 25 miles north of New York City, and its northernmost stop was Dunkirk, 20 miles southwest of Buffalo. There may have been compelling evidence for running a railway between the two towns, but no one has discovered it before or since.

The line's promotional materials described it as a "stupendous work . . . a grand monument to the enterprise, genius and persevering industry of its energetic and indominatible originators and promoters." The Erie's engineers described it as "two streaks of rust." Accidents were routine, fatalities common. The line had more than 30 accidents in 1852 alone. In one of Erie's worst accidents, 40 people died and 75 were wounded in 1868 when a rail cracked and sent an express train off the tracks near Carr's Rock, New York.

Of course, companies that look horrible now can be said to have tremendous potential. The Erie wasn't one of them.

The line had reorganized twice, due to lack of funds, and it probably would have pawned its employees if it could figure out a way to do it. As it was, Erie had four mortgages hanging over it, and Uncle Dan'l owned two of them. Because the company was so far in hock, Erie had issued only one dividend to its long-suffering shareholders. And Drew manipulated the stock so shamelessly that it became known as "The Scarlet Woman of Wall Street."

To handle all the debt, Erie, like many railroads, issued convertible bonds. Bonds are interest-paying IOUs, backed by the company's credit. Convertible bonds can be transformed into common stock at the bearer's demand. By 1867, investors had converted millions into stock, to the point where there was some $25 million of Erie stock floating around. That was big money in those days, the equivalent of several times that today.

Why would Drew or Vanderbilt, canny if unscrupulous men, want to be involved in Erie? Drew's interest in the road was fairly straightforward: He made a fortune from playing the stock, mainly by using Little's technique of selling short when the stock fell. As the company's treasurer, he was privy to inside information that made speculation in its stock much easier. The fact that Drew had this edge—or that he also ran a steamboat company that competed with Erie at points—didn't seem to bother him. "If you own the cow, you own the milk," Drew once said.

Vanderbilt, on the other hand, was bent on building a railway monopoly in much the same way he'd gotten a hammerlock on the steamboat business on the Hudson. The Erie posed competition to his New York Central line, and the Commodore didn't like competition. It ruined things, somehow.

Although he later denied trying to manipulate Erie, Vanderbilt owned an awful lot of it by the fall of 1867. It was just irresistible to him. Whenever he wasn't racing horses in Harlem or driving competitors out of business, he'd stop by his brokers' offices and snap up some more Erie. Practically before he knew it, Vanderbilt had a major stake in the stock.

The Commodore had been on the Erie board of directors for several years—ironically, at Drew's invitation—but rarely showed up for its meetings. But his interest in the company began to perk up as more and more of the stock piled up in his offices. Vanderbilt soon became deeply concerned about the way Drew and his cronies were running the Erie. It was a shame, he'd say, the way the Erie was being run. Some associates of Vanderbilt—who, by pure serendipity, also had big blocks of Erie stock—agreed. It was remarkable how quickly people agreed with Vanderbilt. At any rate, they decided that Drew and his associates should be thrown out and more honest, progressive management be put in—management of the type pioneered by Cornelius Vanderbilt.

So the first battle of Erie was on. Vanderbilt and his associates teamed up against Drew and the rest of the Erie board for the company's annual meeting. Corporations then, as now, adhered to democratic principles: one share, one vote. If you want, you can assign your vote to another shareholder, by allowing that person to vote by proxy. In a frenzy of democratic sentiment, Drew and Vanderbilt proceeded to buy other shareholders' proxies in brisk trading.

Drew had assigned the job of acquiring proxies to one Frederick Lane, who demanded a fee for the service. In an unusual slipup for a man as calculating as Uncle Dan'l, Drew refused to pay Lane's fee. Lane promptly sold the proxies to Vanderbilt, who, as he later noted in a hearing about the matter, had some loose money at the time. To make matters worse for Drew, rumor had it that Vanderbilt was preparing an injunction that would prevent the Old

Bear from keeping some 57,000 Erie shares he'd acquired for an earlier loan to Erie.

It didn't take Drew long to realize that Vanderbilt and his allies would soon be taking over the Erie board. So he screwed up his courage, put on his best face in the midst of adversity, and begged and pleaded with Vanderbilt to let him stay on.

The Commodore was not one easily moved by whining, as Drew well knew: The last time he had tried the tactic with Vanderbilt, he wound up several million dollars poorer. But something must have touched the Commodore this time, if only the thought of his opponent's shameless groveling. At any rate, Vanderbilt relented. The Commodore had terms, though: Drew was to stop manipulating Erie stock, unless, of course, he let the Commodore in on the plans first. Vanderbilt's allies were shocked and outraged at the deal until they figured out that Drew and the Commodore could outvote them. Then they decided it was a pretty good idea after all.

At the Erie elections, the Vanderbilt forces swept out the old guard, including Drew. The business community hailed the changes in Erie, and the major papers heralded the dawn of a new era for the road. The next day's dawning, however, saw one Vanderbilt man resign, for health reasons, no doubt. Daniel Drew was named to take his place and was given his old job of treasurer back.

Two other individuals of note appeared on the Erie board. One was James Fisk, who, appropriately, started his career working for a circus. (In an interesting twist of fate, Drew had spent three of his early years in a circus as well.) He briefly assisted Drew in his steamboat business, and when the Civil War erupted, Fisk answered his nation's call by running cotton through the Union blockade for his employer, Boston's Jordan, Marsh & Company He also profited handsomely by some private sales of defective blankets to the Union. Not that Fisk, a Vermont native, had any love for the Stars and Bars. On the day Lee met Grant at the Appomattox Courthouse, Fisk allegedly hired a fast boat, sailed to England, and sold some $5 million in Confederate bonds before the news of the surrender arrived. At the end of hostilities, he began speculating on Wall Street, went broke, found more capital in Boston, and eventually founded the brokerage house of Fisk & Belden.

In character, Fisk was a cross between Willard Scott and Donald Trump. He loved attention, odd costumes, bad jokes, and opulence. In return for financial assistance to a local military unit, Fisk got an honorary colonelship, and would lead parades and maneuvers in full regalia. He once led an unsuccessful foray to quell a neighborhood distur- bance and was chased through back yards and over fences across several blocks by irate citizens. From time to time— particularly when on board a steamboat—he'd don an ad- miral's uniform. "If Vanderbilt's a commodore, then I'm an admiral," he once said. When not impersonating military officers, Fisk liked sumptuous meals at Delmonico's, drink- ing champagne, and wearing expensive jewelry.

Unlike Scott, however, Fisk also had a taste for bud- ding young starlets, many of whom had day jobs in board- ing houses with unusually liberal visitation rules. They didn't seem to mind his large size, boorishness, or modest personal fortune. Fisk's wife, who would have been over- whelmed by the corruption of New York City, remained in their Boston mansion at his insistence.

The other new member of the Erie board was a young broker named Jay Gould, who later went on to become one of the most hated men in America. Gould's more recent biographers argue that he was probably no worse than the rest of the crowd on Wall Street at the time—just smarter, and that much of his bad press was sour grapes. There may be some truth to this, but, on the other hand, when people spend all that time and energy hating you, there could be a grain of truth behind it. (Cornelius Vanderbilt: "[Gould is] a damned villain.")

By the age of 23, Gould had already run a tannery, built a cord road, surveyed several counties in New York, written a history of another, and promoted a better mouse-trap. I suppose if he'd had the time, he would have built a better mousetrap as well. Later on he dabbled in trading hides, but left when his partner killed himself. Gould's partner probably would have killed himself anyway, but being around Gould didn't help matters much. (Daniel Drew: "His touch is death.")

Gould was very good to his family, which was fortunate because he was rotten to everyone else. A gaunt, hollow-eyed man, Gould became gaunter and hollower as he hatched his schemes. After one particularly audacious effort to corner the gold market, Jim Fisk described him as "just a heap of clothes and a pair of eyeballs." Fisk probably would have added that Gould was surrounded by tiny bits of paper, because Gould liked to shred paper while his plans unfolded. (Henry Adams: [Gould] had not a conception of a moral principle.")

Nevertheless, Gould and Fisk became fast friends and one of the oddest couples in history. The shy and reserved Gould, one can assume, lived vicariously through Fisk's clowning and buffoonery. And while Fisk often played the fool, those who brushed into him on the market quickly found out that he was one of the sharpest operators on the Street. Before a year had passed, Wall Street would find out just how sharp Fisk and Gould really were. (Trumbull White: "At the time the Gould-Fisk ring was sucking the life-blood of the Erie, the Tweed-Sweeny ring was plundering the city of New York. The two were really one.")

At any rate, the Erie election marked a standoff in the war. Vanderbilt, at least nominally, had won control of Erie and assumed that Drew's manipulations would end, as would Erie's periodic rate wars with his New York Central line. Drew, on the other hand, still had his inside information and was free to speculate in the stock, provided he didn't interfere with the Commodore's game plan.

Vanderbilt really should have known better. Drew, though never a magnetic personality, hit it off extremely well with the other members of the board, and strange things began happening. For example, Vanderbilt and his cronies formed a pool in late 1867 to buy some $9 million of Erie stock. In Wall Street parlance, this is called "bulling the stock." Heavy buying in one particular stock often attracts more money, driving the price even higher. Drew was to manage the pool.

Peculiarly, Erie didn't rise. Uncle Dan'l appeared puzzled, but offered encouragement. "Keep on buying, boys, she's certain to rise," he told his fellow pool members. "Don't be scared." As the rest of the market soared, Erie stayed at virtually the same price, sinking promptly whenever it started to rise. The pool members became suspicious and began to wonder who, exactly, was selling all that stock to them. After some investigation, the other pool members discovered that the seller was Daniel Drew. The Old Bear offered some of his profits to the pool, but it was probably far from an equal division.

This was the sort of joke that Vanderbilt could take, since he and Drew had been clipping each other for years. I suppose if they hadn't been multimillionaires, they would have stolen each other's porch steps and laughed their heads off. But Drew's behavior didn't improve much after that. Erie started negotiating connections with other railroads, an action which would have threatened Vanderbilt's cherished monopolies. This raised the grim specter of competition, that enemy of free enterprise, and Vanderbilt decided that enough was enough.

In February 1868, Frank Work, Erie's new director, applied for an injunction to make Drew return the 57,000 shares of Erie he'd received for making a loan to the line in 1866. Curiously, the injunction was almost the same as the one his uncle, Cornelius Vanderbilt, had threatened to use against Drew just a year before. Work applied for the injunction from New York State Supreme Court Judge George Barnard, a Tammany Hall hack who could often think of thousands of good reasons for favoring the rich and particularly Vanderbilt. Barnard approved the injunction. Three days later, Barnard approved another of Work's injunctions, removing Drew from Erie's board.

At some point, either just before or after the first injunction, someone devised a plan that would get you or me thrown into prison if we even thought about it. Drew is generally given credit for the plot, but most agree that it sounds like something Jay Gould would cook up. (Joseph Pulitzer: "[Gould is] one of the most sinister figures that has ever flitted bat-like across the vision of the American people.")

The plan was actually relatively simple. The Erie plotters knew that Vanderbilt had standing orders to buy all the Erie stock available. The Erie's executive committee, on the other hand, had the power to issue new stock, indirectly at least, by issuing convertible bonds that could be transformed into stock almost instantly. So Drew and the rest of the committee would flood the market with new Erie stock. The proceeds from the stock sales would go out of Vanderbilt's pockets and into the Erie treasury.

But just selling Vanderbilt stock wasn't good enough for Drew and company. On Wall Street, when a company issues more stock without any particular improvement in the company's prospects, the stock generally nosedives. Since the company is essentially the same, a larger supply of shares simply means that each share is worth less. Knowing this, the Erie directors planned to make a fortune by going short.

It's probably a good idea to say a bit more about the short sale at this point. When you sell short, you borrow shares from someone else—generally your broker—and sell them, hoping to buy the shares back at a lower price. Suppose, for example, you borrowed 1,000 shares of Erie from your broker and sold it on the open market at $80 per share. If the shares fell to $70, you could buy enough at $70 to repay your broker, and pocket the $10 per share difference. There are two problems with this strategy. The first is that the stock can rise, forcing you to buy back your shares at a loss. And while a stock can only fall by 100 percent—to zero—there's no end to how far it can rise. The other is that if someone owns all the shares when you need to pay back your borrowed shares, that person can ask any price at all for the shares you need. This is called a "short squeeze," and it was considered a laugh riot to squeeze the shorts in Drew's day. Drew, who had squeezed his share of shorts, even composed a small poem on the matter:

> He who sells what isn't his'n
> Buys it back or goes to prison.

The vehicle for the Vanderbilt sting was Erie's executive board, which consisted of Drew, Gould, Fisk, and another major stockholder, John Eldridge, who was easily as reptilian as the other three. Frank Work, Vanderbilt's man, was also on the board, but the Drew clique was able to outvote him. The executive board could meet at any time in order to be able to deal with emergencies. This was a fortunate and far-sighted provision of the company's charter, because an emergency cropped up right after Work's first injunction was served. The Erie's rail supervisor came to the executive board, decrying the line's appalling condition and asking for millions of dollars' worth of improvements. Just one year before, the same man had noted, approvingly, that the Erie's physical plant was in the best condition it had seen for 10 years. The executive committee, shocked by the railroad's sudden deterioration, voted to issue $10 million in convertible bonds for those improvements.

The committee promptly converted half the bonds to stock, which Drew dumped on the market. Vanderbilt bought them. The committee then converted the remaining bonds to stock before the second injunction hit, at which point Drew was unable to act as a company officer. The 50,000 shares sat in Drew's broker's safe, and the Old Bear and his faction let the market stew for the next 10 days.

Drew's brokers then dumped the remaining 50,000 shares on the market. Vanderbilt's men, who had been snapping up all the Erie offered for sale, soon found the market flooded with Erie. The stock started the session of February 29, 1868, in the 70s and started sinking rapidly. When Erie hit 68¾, Drew offered some sympathy for Vanderbilt. "I'm really sorry for Vanderbilt," Drew said, "but he oughtn't to be so rash. A man of his years ought to know better than to fly in the face of Providence. I pity him, indeed I do; and I hope this blessed day will be a lesson to him." The stock bottomed at 65.

Vanderbilt's response, if any, has been lost to posterity. At one point, however, one of his brokers asked if he should start to sell Erie. "Sell?" the Commodore roared. "You fool, no! Buy all the shares offered!" And buy he did, to the tune of some $3.5 million of Erie. By the end of the day, Erie was propped back up to the low 70s.

Vanderbilt was still in control, but it was a Pyrrhic victory at best: The Commodore now owned a huge amount of Erie stock that hadn't been around before, and maintaining the stock price was a strain even for Vanderbilt. Unless he kept buying all the stock issued, Erie's price would plummet, probably taking Vanderbilt and the rest of the New York Stock Exchange with it.

The fact that Vanderbilt owned so much of the outrageously diluted stock didn't mean he was happy about it. He used the good offices of Judge Barnard to order Erie to stop issuing new stock and to stop making agreements with other railroads. The order also enjoined Drew from buying or selling any Erie stock until the matter of the 57,000 shares was settled.

This was bad news for the bears. To make matters worse, Drew's short contracts were soon coming due. (In those days, short contracts had settlement dates. In today's enlightened market, you can keep losing money as long as you have some left.) Although he didn't own all the Erie shares—that would be too steep even for a man of the Commodore's means—Vanderbilt was able to keep the price high enough to make the bears' settlement dates extremely uncomfortable.

But once again, Vanderbilt had underestimated Drew, as well as Gould and Fisk, who seemed to amplify the Speculative Director's instincts. Drew was intimately familiar with the New York judicial system, primarily because lawsuits seemed to follow him wherever he went. Drew knew, for example, that New York State Supreme Court judges were on equal footing on some matters, and that one judge could order an injunction in conflict with another's. So the Old Bear sent Fisk and Gould off to Binghamton, New York, where an obliging judge issued an injunction against Vanderbilt's man, Work. (The Erie, incidentally, just happened to employ a fair amount of people in Binghamton.) The order also stayed Barnard's orders until all parties could appear before the Erie's judge.

Thus armed with the majesty of the law, the Erie board of directors issued another $5 million of convertible bonds, which Drew bought and converted, through somewhat questionable legal means, to stock. At the same time, Drew enlisted a small army of lawyers to prepare a sheaf of anti-Vanderbilt injunctions.

On Monday, March 9, 1868, Drew's short contracts came due, and the bears brought out their heavy artillery. On the legal front, the Erie clique found another obliging Supreme Court justice (New York had 33 of them) to issue yet another injunction against the Vanderbilt camp. This one, on behalf of Fisk's brokerage partner, William Belden, charged Vanderbilt and his associates, including Judge Barnard, with the heinous crime of manipulating Erie stock. The judge's orders overrode Barnard's previous injunction and allowed Erie to convert yet more bonds into stock.

On the floor of the Exchange, however, Vanderbilt's brokers were keeping the heat on the bears by driving up the price of Erie to 83. Drew had contracts to deliver Erie at 70, meaning he was to take a $13 per share haircut on his short contracts. Fisk, who held the 50,000 shares, was supposed to dump them on the market, depressing the price enough for Drew to get out of his short contract at a profit. As the day wore on, however, Fisk was nowhere to be found. Eventually, Drew became so nervous that he ordered his shorts to be covered at a loss. The second Drew ordered his brokers to buy, Fisk sold—saddling Drew with a large loss on the transaction. This was Fisk's idea of a ripping practical joke.

When Fisk sold, however, the Exchange was once again awash with Erie shares, and even the stoutest Vanderbilt supporters started to quail. In the end, they screwed up their courage, put their best faces on in the midst of adversity, and deserted Vanderbilt by selling. Erie dropped over 10 points, to the low 70s.

Vanderbilt's reaction to the new shares has been lost, probably because his language, when enraged, could crack rock. It is an enduring irony that his name has been linked in the public's mind with his great-granddaughter Amy's book on etiquette. The Commodore didn't waver, however, and under the weight of his indomitable will—as well as his large fortune—Erie stabilized at 77¾. Drew and company, while smarting somewhat from their short contracts, still had about $7 million from the proceeds of Erie stock in the company coffers. The vast bulk of that sum, it can safely be assumed, came from Cornelius Vanderbilt.

The next day, Erie stock slid modestly, but Vanderbilt remained firm. Both sides, at this point, were under so many court injunctions that breathing was probably against court orders. So they did pretty much as they liked.

What Drew liked to do was make Vanderbilt uncomfortable, so he and his allies initiated a "greenback lockup." Before the creation of the Federal Reserve, the nation's money supply was at the mercy of the amount of cash the local banks had on hand. In October, for example, New York banks generally didn't have a lot of money to lend. The reason? Small banks in the South and West called in their loans so they would have enough money for farmers to make their crop settlements. So each October, as cash became scarce, interest rates would soar. High rates made it harder to borrow to buy stocks (most speculators borrowed to invest) and generally had a depressing effect on the stock market.

Drew had discovered that it wasn't hard to take money out of circulation. (He probably learned the trick from Little.) All you have to do is write large, guaranteed checks from accounts on several major banks. The banks had to keep enough cash on hand to cover the checks, in case they should be presented. That money was, effectively, out of circulation, leading to higher rates and a great deal of pressure on people who might need to borrow money to buy more stock—people like Cornelius Vanderbilt, for instance. So Drew and his followers locked up about $7 million, creating a very tight money picture indeed for the Commodore, who needed to borrow money in order to support the Erie's stock.

Vanderbilt went to his bankers, who were now not only short of cash but well aware of the Commodore's current discomforts in the stock market. With the infuriating logic of bankers, they told Vanderbilt that they were reluctant to lend against his now-considerable Erie holdings. It's not good banking practice, after all, to lend against collateral whose value is declining.

Vanderbilt wasn't above using threats to get his way, and this time proved no exception: He threatened to dump all of his shares of the New York Central line on the market. Vanderbilt's bankers all had large blocks of Central in their portfolios, and a precipitous drop in that stock could have swept several banks away. The bankers reflected for a second and then decided Vanderbilt was a pretty good credit risk after all.

So over the next few days, Vanderbilt held the market for Erie aloft while Drew and company held Vanderbilt's $7 million. Vanderbilt, to his credit, didn't flinch. He would stop by his offices, look at the stacks of Erie piling up everywhere, then mosey off to play whist with his buddies. (Cards and fast horses were the Commodore's chief vices, although he probably had others, as evidenced by his second marriage to a woman 40 years his junior.)

Somewhere along the line, however, Vanderbilt or one of his many cronies paid another visit to Judge Barnard, a man who never saw a Vanderbilt injunction he didn't like.

Barnard also had a bone to pick with Uncle Dan'l and the boys: One of the numerous injunctions they had slapped on the Vanderbilt faction actually enjoined Barnard. So Barnard issued a warrant for the arrest of the Erie executive board.

When word reached Drew and company that they were about to be thrown in jail, they did what any other upstanding members of the financial community would do: They stuffed their pockets with greenbacks, grabbed the corporate records, and fled to New Jersey. Gould and Fisk, in a display of bravado, returned to New York that night for a meal at Delmonico's. They skipped out of dinner (and, presumably, the tab) when word arrived that the police were on their way to send the pair to the pokey. The small boat they commandeered at the docks got lost in the fog and was very nearly smashed to flinders by a passing ferry.

By midnight, all three were holed up in the Taylor, a Jersey City hotel. The local press, which had been following the Erie war avidly, quickly nicknamed it "Fort Taylor," and with good reason. A rumor developed that New York City toughs were coming to kidnap Drew. Jersey City called out the police force. And Fisk, never one to make a halfhearted gesture, hired a small army to defend the hotel. Fisk had Erie detectives roam Jersey City and had three cannons mounted on the docks. When rumors of the plot again surfaced, Fisk had more than 125 men guarding the hotel itself. He was even able to drum up armed volunteers from the Jersey countryside.

Whether the guards were necessary or not is debatable. Although there were some decidedly thuglike characters hanging around the Erie depot from time to time, no one has ever proven that Vanderbilt hired them. They could have missed their connection at Piermont. And, in fact, some of them could have been the guards that Fisk had hired.

At first, the conspirators busied themselves in exile. They slashed the fares on Erie and drummed up as much sentiment against Vanderbilt's railroad monopolies. Their lawyers threw a few more injunctions against Vanderbilt and Judge Barnard. They petitioned—and received permission—to have the Erie move its corporate headquarters to New Jersey.

Most importantly, they introduced a bill in the New York state legislature to approve the Erie's dubious bond sales. The legislature was willing to hear arguments from both sides. Most legislators, in fact, were willing to hear thousands of arguments from both sides. Vanderbilt won the early bidding by bribing the Erie representative, who disappeared with at least enough cash to give $1,000 to each legislator. The New York House of Representatives committee pondering the Erie's bill delivered a negative report by a large majority.

The Senate, however, was also investigating the bill, and a Senator journeyed to Jersey to chat with Drew, Fisk, and Gould. Most of the chat revolved around the poor pay that senators received. So Jay Gould packed some clothes and several hundred thousand dollars and headed off to New York, where he was promptly arrested. Gould posted the $500,000 bail and made his appearance in court, where he was released in the charge of a court officer.

The officer followed Gould to his hotel room, where he began packing his bags and arranging to take the night train to Albany. "But you're supposed to be in my custody," the guard exclaimed. "Well, then, come with me to Albany, and I'll still be in your custody," Gould replied. This seemed logical to the guard at the time, so they both traveled north.

Once in Albany, Gould's health deteriorated rapidly, to the point where his physician said it was impossible for him to return to New York. Apparently, the only cure for

Gould's condition was visiting the statehouse and handing out large sums to legislators, lobbyists, and newspaper editors, because that is precisely what he did.

Gould's largess was impressive, even for those heady days, and Vanderbilt quit the field in disgust. The legislature, hoping for several thousand more arguments from the Commodore, was furious. Of the 106 votes cast on the Erie bill, only five were against it. The legislators even passed three anti-Vanderbilt bills for good measure.

During this entire time, the Erie conspirators were obliged to stay in New Jersey, since the wrath of Judge Barnard still hung over New York. Fisk, ever the one to make the best of a bad situation, brought his mistress, Josie Mansfield, over to the hotel to make it more homey. He also plied the local press with food, drink, and cigars while noting that the Erie war was beneficial to the poor, somehow. Gould, a good family man and shy of the limelight, was decidedly uncomfortable, although he did manage to choke down the roast quail and pheasant dinners at the hotel.

Drew, on the other hand, was miserable. Despite the fact that he had the ethics of a cat, he'd never been a fugitive before. He missed his wife and his children, as well as Wall Street, where he could spend happy hours fleecing the unwary. And oddly enough, Drew was a devout Methodist, and high living and fancy women honestly made him uncomfortable. If Drew were alive today, you can bet he wouldn't be driving a Mercedes or wearing suspenders.

New York law forbade imprisoning people on civil charges on Sundays, so Drew and Gould would return home on the Sabbath, while Fisk would make the New York rounds. Ever mindful of Drew's methods, however, Fisk and Gould hired a detective to tail Drew. The detective quickly discovered that Drew's strolls took him to Vanderbilt's house, where, according to rumor, the two were deep in peace negotiations.

Fisk and Gould confronted Drew about this and reminded him of his agreement to split the proceeds from the Vanderbilt sting with them. Drew blithely informed them that, as treasurer, he had made arrangements for the Erie's funds to return to New York. Just as coolly, Fisk told Drew that he had attached Drew's cash through an obliging New Jersey judge. Drew fell silent and paced the floor for a few minutes. "Well, Jeems, I see you're as keen as you need to be," he said, after a moment. "How can we compromise?" Not surprisingly, Erie's treasury returned to Jersey.

Despite the discovery, Drew continued to negotiate with Vanderbilt, and hostilities between both sides cooled down considerably. By the end of April 1868, Fort Taylor was deserted. By July, the settlement with Vanderbilt was complete, with some $4.5 million going to the Commodore and the rest being divided up among various other lawyers, operators, and politicians.

Jay Gould and Jim Fisk received no cash for their part in the Great Erie War but inherited the burnt-out shell of the company. They invited Boss Tweed, the unbelievably corrupt manager of Tammany Hall, onto the board of directors and milked the company for several more years, issuing yet more stock. When Tweed was finally arrested, Fisk and Gould were driven out of the management. Gould was removed forcibly from the Erie offices by a committee of outraged shareholders, among whom numbered no less than General Sheridan, late of Civil War fame.

Jay Gould went on to corner the gold market (dumping his accomplice, Fisk, at a critical moment), build railroad and communications monopolies, and generally make everyone hate him even more. After an irritated speculator dumped him over the rails of a basement barber shop, he kept a bodyguard about him at all times. He died with an $80 million fortune.

Fisk died of lead poisoning not long after the gold corner. Josie Mansfield had found herself a lover, who shot Fisk to death. He left about $1 million to his long-suffering wife in Boston and a collection of 250 birds. His funeral outshone Little's and came close to showing up Lincoln's. He was 36 years old.

Cornelius Vanderbilt lived another nine years, dying on January 3, 1877, with some $80 million in the bank. His descendants squandered the bulk of his fortune, with many having only his name as their legacy.

The Erie limped on. The cash from the Vanderbilt settlement came, of course, from its treasury rather than from the pockets of anyone concerned. Erie shareholders didn't see a dividend for another 63 years. (Eventually, the road was absorbed by the Penn Central, which went spectacularly bankrupt in the 1960s.)

Daniel Drew lost his position on the Erie board as a result of the settlement, although he kept his considerable profits from his private operations in the stock. His fortunes before and after the Erie war are chronicled in the illustrative section that follows.

THE BOOK ON DANIEL DREW

Daniel Drew must have had a lovable side to him. Otherwise, he would have been lynched early on.[1]

Drew was the son of Gilbert Drew and his second wife, Catherine Muckleworth. He was born in Putnam County, New York, on July 29, 1797, on Gilbert Drew's farm. At that time, Putnam County, while not the frontier, was wild country and not terribly well-suited for farming.[2] As a boy, helping his aging father clear land and plant crops, Drew decided he wasn't meant for farming.[3]

Life on the farm left little time for much else, and Drew's schooling was minimal.[4] On this score, he was little different from most men of his time. In rascality, however, he stood head and shoulders above the rest.

When the War of 1812 broke out, Drew and his brother quickly came to their country's aid. They sold themselves as substitutes and later deserted.[5]

---

[1]People may have tried, but we don't know that.
[2]It's not at this time, either.
[3]Hauling rocks will do that to you.
[4]Drew was semiliterate at best. He spelled *door* d-o-a-r.
[5]Both later came back, though.

When the war was over, Drew returned to Putnam County and became a drover, bringing sheep, cattle, and other animals from the country into New York City. His first herds were probably "bob sheep." The trick with driving bob sheep is to make sure they die just after you sell them, not before.[6]

In the middle of his droving career, he came down with a severe case of Methodism that was to plague him all his life. His mother, a devout Baptist, probably gave him considerable religous instruction; it wasn't until he attended a Methodist revival, however, that he got religion.[7]

His life as a drover—and, at one point, as a carnival shill—tended to put his religious instincts at odds with his utterly reptilian financial instincts. It caused him a great many heartaches, but he found that repenting was a great deal easier with a wad of money in his pocket.

Once, when on a drive from the farms of Putnam to the meat markets of the Bowery, Drew had a revelation. As he and his horses were sitting under a tree during a thunderstorm, the tree was hit by lightning and Drew got a pretty big charge out of it, too. When he came to, he discovered his horse had been driven to that big pasture in the sky. He decided it was God's way of warning him to stay on the path of religion.[8]

His religious beliefs aside (which they often were), Drew soon proved himself a shrewd trader, and stories about his deals began to grow around him.[9] Supposedly,

---

[6]As with most things, timing is everything in the bob sheep trade.

[7]Compared to what else was going on in Putnam County, a Methodist revival was pretty exciting.

[8]Others have argued that it was God's way of frying a horse.

[9]Only some of them were true.

Drew once approached Henry Astor, John Jacob Astor's brother, about buying some livestock. Astor, at this time, was the foremost butcher in New York and a keen judge of cowflesh. Henry liked what he saw—a herd of fat beefsteak—and paid top dollar for them.

What Astor didn't know was that Drew, for the past three days, hadn't allowed the cattle to drink. In fact, he'd thrown salt in with their feed at night and driven them—out of their minds with thirst—to New York. Just before the approach to Astor's farm, there was a stream, where Drew let them drink their fill. The water added many pounds to the cattle, and their bloated bellies looked like fat to Astor.[10]

That night, as Drew rode back to Putnam, the cows felt the call of nature, and reverted to their scrawny selves. Astor, viewing the herd, shouted "I've been sold watered stock!"

As the story goes, Astor then shut up, and when Drew came back to town with another herd of fat cattle to sell, Astor told his main competitor to buy Drew's wonderful beef. This continued until every butcher in New York had been taken in.

Drew's biographer points out, correctly, that the story is pure balderdash.[11] In fact, the story has its roots in folklore so old it was a knee-slapper when people were still in the trees. Nevertheless, it shows how good a trader Drew was.

Drew had married Roxanna Meade when he was 25 and beginning to feel the urge to settle down. So he became proprietor of the Bull's Head Tavern, where the drovers came to sell their herds on Tuesdays and Thursdays.[12]

---

[10]No one ever accused Astor of being too smart for his own good.

[11]Drew watered the kind of stock that had no legs.

[12]Methodists were opposed to drinking. Drew apparently discovered a loophole.

Running the Bull's Head gave him some ready cash, and he began looking about for a place to invest it. Like most New Yorkers of the time, he had seen one of the biggest and earliest business battles of that island's history: How a young upstart from Queens, Cornelius Vanderbilt, had broken the steamboat monopoly held by Robert Fulton on the Hudson. Vanderbilt had used a simple tactic: He undercut Fulton's fares dramatically and, by buying off the press, launched a massive campaign portraying himself as the champion of the people against the evil Fulton monopoly.[13]

Drew admired Vanderbilt's technique and promptly bought a rusting hulk named The Water Witch. He then proceeded to take passengers up the Hudson for a fraction of Vanderbilt's fares, naming his steamship company The People's Line and proclaiming his opposition to the Vanderbilt monopoly.

This continued for nearly a year, and Drew lost some $10,000 on the People's Line. He did win, however, the love of the people—which he promptly betrayed by agreeing to match rates with the Commodore.[14]

Drew maintained his steamboat business for nearly 20 years thereafter, even after the railroad business had clearly sounded the death knell of the Hudson River. More importantly, however, he started a successful banking business that lasted another 10 years until one of his partners died.

By this time, Drew was a wealthy man. "I was wonderfully blessed at money-making," Drew would say the year he died. "I got to be a millionaire before I knowed it, hardly."

---

[13]Anyone who knew Cornelius must have busted a gut laughing.
[14]Vanderbilt gave him several thousand very good reasons to do so.

His fortune approached $15 million, eventually—a tidy sum in those days.[15]

During the panic and ensuing depression of 1857, Drew managed to get elected to the directorship of the Erie Railroad, the upshot of which is detailed in Chapter 3. In the days before the Great Erie War, however, Drew's sharp trading—and penchant for treachery—became legendary. He pioneered the use of options in trading, for example; and, when the trades went against him, he wasn't above trying to wriggle out of his obligations. Occasionally, his brokers would override him and sell out his position anyway.

Despite Drew's reputation as being utterly untrustworthy, however, Wall Street took a shine to him. Unlike Gould, who was universally hated and required a bodyguard at all times, Drew wasn't threatened by those he sheared. People thought of him as "smart."[16] People probably also liked his tendency to pick on the rich. It was a sort of compulsion with him.

When Drew lost his inside position on the Erie, he lost some of his legendary business savvy—and some of his sense, since he took a short position against the Erie when Fisk and Gould were bulling the stock. He tried his usual whining and cajoling when he was caught short by Fisk and Drew, but to no avail. They took him for $1.5 million.

Drew's fortunes continued to sink until he was caught in the panic of 1873 and forced to declare bankruptcy. His assets were listed as $150, including a family Bible and a seal greatcoat. He retired for a while to Putnam County, but

---

[15]It's not bad these days, either.

[16]Back then, the word had more of a connotation of "cunning" rather than "intelligent."

found it uncomfortable there.[17] He eventually moved in with his son and in 1879 died unremarked by the rest of Wall Street.

AFTERWORD

The Great Erie War is probably the best-known of all the episodes of financial chicanery in this book. Nevertheless, it's known primarily to people who study Wall Street lore. Drew himself sank into relative obscurity by the time of his death, only to rise to brief notoriety through the publication of Bouk White's *The Book of Daniel Drew*. White's book was nearly complete fiction, however, and only recently— through Clifford Browder's remarkable biography of Drew—have all the details of Drew's tumultuous life become relatively clear.

Drew's outrageous behavior, particularly in light of his apparently heartfelt Methodism, still remains somewhat endearing. Unlike the robber barons of the 1980s, such as Michael Milkin, Ivan Boesky, and Charles Keating, Drew had a certain homespun guile that makes him, if not lovable, at least marvelously entertaining. Perhaps the fact that he tended to cheat fellow millionaires, rather than ordinary investors (usually) is his saving grace.

Drew's relationship with Commodore Vanderbilt is perhaps the most unusual aspect of the entire episode. Both men competed fiercely to control the Hudson steamboat lines and earned a peculiar affection for each other. Even when Drew was bankrupt living on his son's charity in Putnam County, he had only kind words for Cornele.

---

[17]People kept pestering him about money they'd lent him to buy bob sheep. He'd forgotten all about it.

The story of the Great Erie war was first recounted in a systematic way by Charles Francis Adams, who used the episode for a philippic on the entire age. Other chroniclers, however, reflected the general admiration for Fisk and Drew—they were smart and unscrupulous, and those were characteristics admired in those days. Gould, for numerous reasons, never attracted much in the way of admiring press.

SELECTED BIBLIOGRAPHY

Adams, Charles Francis. *Chapters of Erie.* Ithaca, N.Y.: Cornell University Press, 1968. A reprint of Adams's lengthy 1871 treatment of the Erie war, worth reading if only for the sheer acid content of its analysis.

Browder, Clifford. *The Money Game in Old New York: Daniel Drew and His Times.* Lexington: The University Press of Kentucky, 1986. Browder not only wrote the definitive biography of Drew, but draws on a myriad of sources to create a fabulous picture of New York in Drew's day.

Klein, Maury. *The Life and Legend of Jay Gould.* Baltimore: The Johns Hopkins Press, 1986. If anything about Jay Gould has been left out of this book, it's probably not worth bothering with.

McAlpine, R. W. *The Life and Times of Col. James Fisk, Jr.* New York, 1872. Although probably packed with lies, a ripping account of Fisk's life.

White, Bouk. *The Book of Daniel Drew.* New York: Arno Press, 1970. Written in 1910, White's book was nearly a complete fraud—a fitting tribute to Drew in its own way.

CHAPTER 4

SONG OF THE SWAMP

If you've ever spent a winter north of Baltimore, you know why some Swedes stroll down the street puffing on a stick of dynamite instead of a Corona Grenadier. In the dead heat of summer, you may fantasize about lying in front of the fire on a bearskin rug while the winter wind howls about the cabin. What you don't think about is trying to start the car when the wind chill is 40 degrees below zero, or the fact that no matter how many clothes you wear, your nose still hurts. The reason why the cradle of mankind is Africa and not International Falls, Minnesota, is because people don't have much in the way of fur, and frostbite would have deprived our ancestors of one of our major evolutionary features, the opposable thumb.

If you think winters are uncomfortable now, think how they must have been in 1923, when central heating often meant that there were holes in the first-floor ceilings that allowed heat from the downstairs to filter up eventually. Consider the fact that many people still didn't have outdoor plumbing, which meant trotting out to an unheated outhouse during cold snaps. Cogitate about the fact that the car heaters in those days were few and far between and that horses didn't have any to speak of. Now you know why your parents (or grandparents) always say how much warmer it is these days.

Even the most hard-core winter fanatics—the kind whose idea of a great time is camping atop New Hampshire's Mount Washington in February—admit that the thrill of newly fallen snow is diminished somewhat in mid-April. Around that time, when the miracle of daffodils in bloom is nearly always bushwhacked by a late frost, the lure of the tropics looms large. In 1923, the lure of the tropics, and particularly Florida, began to reach epic proportions. It was then that the fabled Florida land boom began, and in two short years it had captured the imagination of America. Within another year, the Florida land boom had passed into American folklore, a byword for greed and gullibility.

As 1923 began, there were all sorts of perfectly good reasons for buying Florida land. First of all, it was cheap, relatively speaking. Florida land prices had done little since the turn of the century—and for good reason.

Although Miami today is now one of the nation's most populous and important cities, it got a late start in life. Even though Florida boasts the oldest settlement in the continental New World—Saint Augustine—Miami wasn't settled until the 1870s, when it grew up around the site of Fort Dallas, an outpost in the Seminole Wars. The city really didn't get rolling until 1896, when Henry Flagler, a Northerner, extended the Florida East Coast Railway to Miami and began promoting it as a vacation spot.

Despite Flagler's promotions, Miami still didn't amount to much by the early 1920s. The main reason was that there wasn't any burning reason to go to Miami.

Most great cities arise because they have some geographical advantage, or because they sit at the crossroads of trade. New York, for example, has one of the greatest harbors in the world—deep, spacious and bustling. Chicago sat upon the crossroads between East and West and drew its population from the movement of commodities across the country.

Miami, on the other hand, had no great boasts to make about geography. It had the Florida climate, but so did the rest of Florida. Cuba had roughly the same climate, and its tourist trade was much further advanced. The Biscayne Bay, though lovely to look at, was shallow and not suited for the big passenger ships that could bring in scads of tourists. In 1923, it could boast only an 18-foot-deep channel for ships, as well as a small area for them to turn back around. The building of an adequate harbor had been hindered for years by the railroad, which had owned virtually all of the harborside until 1920.

Another problem with Miami and environs was that it had no natural water. Fresh water had to be collected from rainfall in cisterns, a practice that tends to make for bountiful mosquito populations and a wide variety of tropical diseases. In addition, while the winter months in south Florida are delightful, the summers are like touring east Hell in a tank.

Furthermore, Miami was the crossroads to nowhere. To the west lay the Everglades, and to the south the Keys studded the Atlantic. These are wonderful areas to visit, but the amount of trade from either area has been negligible for a long time and probably will remain so for some time to come. The area's one great asset was its citrus and avocado groves, but these were hardly enough to bring the world trooping to Miami's doors.

Furthermore, although there were some lovely stretches of beaches near Miami, getting to south Florida was troublesome before the 1920s, to say the least. No passenger ships went directly from the North to Florida until 1923. The Dixie Highway, the only route to Miami, was paved primarily with good intentions. The train was probably the best way into town, but it was still a long trip ways to go for most Americans, and expensive as well.

By the spring of 1923, however, things began to look up for Miami. Technology was one reason. The auto had become more commonplace, thanks primarily to Henry Ford and the Model T. In the early days of motoring in the United States—the previous two decades—you were taking your life into your hands if you went much over 30. This was due partly to the automotive technology of the times but also to the state of the roads, most of which were built with horses and not flivvers in mind. As more people began owning and driving cars, more and better roads were built and driving to Florida became more realistic.

Furthermore, the airplane, or rather the idea of the airplane, fired the imagination of speculators and developers. Although an expensive and impractical—if not dangerous—means of travel in the early 1920s, America saw the airplane for what it was: the transportation of the future. Commercial air service to Florida was some ways off, but it wasn't hard to believe that when it came, Americans would flock to Florida.

Other, more conventional reasons also made Florida land a plausible investment. Since the end of the Great War, inflation had raged, sending up the prices of food and clothing to near-record levels. Adding to the problem was the demobilization of the army, which meant that more men were shedding their uniforms and reentering the work force. Although the postwar economy absorbed the doughboys quite well, the huge pool of men looking for jobs meant that employers could offer low wages and few raises in the years after World War I.

By 1923, however, the situation had stabilized, and, as the pool of unemployed workers dwindled, wages began to catch up with prices. The end result was that workers had not only enough money to spend but enough to make them start thinking about investing as well. What's more, many workers for the first time ever had enough time off to think about long vacations. For those in the North and Midwest, a vacation in Florida became a possibility for the first time.

Finally, the mood of the country underwent a sea change throughout the 1920s. The Great War, which claimed more lives in a single battle than all of the U.S. deaths in Vietnam, had drained the country of nearly every ounce of selflessness it had. In the fever of the war years, Americans had been exhorted to sacrifice: donating money, time, and the lives of its children to the Greater Good. Once the war was over, the country had a bad case of what consumers call "pent-up demand." In more human terms, however, the country had endured a terrible period of hardship and an awful lot of death—not only from the war, but from the plague of influenza that coincided with it. America was ready for a good time.

The best things in life may be free, but you can usually buy an awful lot of fun, provided you have the money. In the years after the war, even as inflation was impoverishing the nation, enough people were making money for the rest of the country to sit up and take notice. Farmland was appreciating smartly as food prices rose, and the stock market began the first leg of a run that was to take it to its rendezvous with the Crash. Those who were making money were "smart," according to the parlance of the day, and, what's more, anyone with enough smarts could get rich, too. If there hadn't been a Florida, someone would have invented one.

The first inklings of the boom began in the spring, when construction loans in Miami began to pick up. Starting in April 1923, building permits in the Miami area began to rise in million-dollar amounts each month, and prices inside Miami began to rise. Meanwhile, the labors of a few pioneers had come to bear fruit.

First and foremost was Miami Beach, once a long strip of mangrove swamp that kept Miami from the wrath of the Atlantic. Legendary developer Carl Fisher turned it into a long, white sand beach and reaped millions in profits. Similar stories, some of them actually true, were told of developers who had taken raw swampland and turned it into playgrounds for the rich and famous. From these true stories were to come the justification, just a few years later, for buying Florida swampland.

The first year of the boom was 1924, and those who invested in Miami then reaped big rewards. As is typical of a land boom, the main activity centered in the city, where rising prices are easier to justify. A project that involves turning vacant lots into hotels in Miami Beach, after all, is an easier sell to investors than a motel, say, smack in the middle of the Everglades.

And there were lots of good stories in the Miami area in 1924. Miami dredged out a large area called Elser Pier at the foot of Flagler Park and created Bayfront Park. A new hotel, the Sweetwater, was begun at a cost of $2 million. Paramount Enterprises started the Miami Theater, which eventually rose to 10 stories. Miami Beach started to boom, too. In 1923, Miami Beach could boast of five hotels and two casinos. Some $4 million in new construction was added in 1923 and another $7 million in 1924.

In September, however, a new twist was added. In 1980s, the twist would be called "synergy"—the concept that the parts of a thing are worth more than the whole. In the last decade, synergy meant buying up a huge company, often by borrowing vast sums, breaking it up, and selling off the parts. If you were lucky, you made more from selling the parts than the fantastic amounts you'd borrowed. If you were unlucky, you filed for Chapter 11 bankruptcy and let the courts do the dividing for you.

In Florida, the concept was similar: Buy up a big tract of land, subdivide it, and sell off the lots for a greater amount than the price of the original lot. It started with a bang in December of 1924. In the north end of Miami, a company called the Shoreland Company pieced together some 2,500 acres of land and announced the creation of Miami Shores. The development was to include a $2 million hotel, but the developers never got around to building it, somehow. They were busy enough as it was, opening opulent offices and renting Cadillacs and touring buses for the staff and eager "prospects."

Shoreland carved 12,000 building sites out of its 2,500 acres. The first round of sales brought in more than $2.5 million. At its peak, Shoreland would sell $30 million—in one round of sales.

Other developments began to appear around Miami at the same time. Also in September 1924, George E. Merrick sold off five lots west of Miami from the site of the Merrick mansion, which was built by his father, a former Congregational minister. The mansion was built of coral, which was abundant in the area, and the minister named it Coral Gables. The sale raised $5,500 in five days.

Unlike most of his fellow developers, George Merrick had a certain amount of taste as well as a good sense of design. Since coral was the most available material, the homes that were to rise at Coral Gables were made of coral quarried locally. Merrick favored a Mediterranean design in architecture, which also made sense, given the south

Florida climate. And, since the land was swampy, he incor-
porated canals into the plan, instantly making a huge hit
across the nation. Developers as far north as Long Island
copied the plan. Coral Gables, however, was not to fully
bloom for another two years.

As development got under way in late 1924, Miami's
main raison d'être, its acres of avocado and citrus groves,
began to disappear. A farm owned by T. A. Winfield by the
bay in Miami, which once sported the champion avocado
tree in South Florida, was ripped down to become Shore
Crest. A citrus grove owned by one George Cellon became
Tierra Alta. A dairy farm owned by a man named Melrose
gave his name to Melrose Gardens and Melrose Heights.

Under the law of supply and demand, prices fall as
supply rises. It didn't work in Florida in 1924. As new developments came onto the market, land prices generally
began to rise. A corner lot in Miami bought for $170,000 in
November sold for $200,000 a month later. Some 2,170
acres north and west of Miami sold for more than $1 mil-
lion, the biggest land sale up to then in Florida history.
Inside what is now Miami, 40 acres sold for $152,000. The
land had sold for $28,000 2 years before and $2.75 an acre
40 years before that. The Florida Cities Finance Company
began touting Fulford-by-the-Sea, a community which, according to its founder, would eventually cost $60 million,
including Fulford University and a million-dollar speedway. The community is now called North Miami Beach, and
both the speedway and the university are still in the planning stages.

Even at this early stage in the boom—the crest was
still a year away—hucksters started to get into the act. A
promoter for a magazine that never existed, called *Happen-
ings in Miami,* offered a free lot in the exciting town of
Flamingo in exchange for a five-year subscription. Those
who looked for their magazine never found it, nor did they

find Flamingo, which was supposedly somewhere between Orlando and Kissimmee. To get a title for the land, however, the subscriber had to pay $15 for the title, which also never appeared.

In the meantime, the sort of pseudodevelopment that was to put Florida land in the lexicon of scams was also on the rise. Lake Okeechobee, for instance, was being described as "The Chicago of South" by the Charles Henck Company. Just what the Chicago of the South would have to import or export from the Everglades was not specified, although a few efforts to grow peanuts and sugar were made there.

Developers, obviously, grew with the boom. So did the newspaper industry. The Miami *Herald* found itself flooded with advertisements, a flood that would turn into a torrent in 1925 and 1926 and launch the paper into the world-class status it enjoys today. At the height of the boom, the *Herald* found itself in a position that would make other newspapers green with envy: larger than any other paper in America and having to turn away advertisers.

Others noticed that the newspaper business could have a dandy potential in the middle of a real estate boom. One was Cornelius Vanderbilt, Jr., the 26-year-old great-grandson of the indomitable Commodore. In October of 1924, Vanderbilt rolled into Miami, promising to build a railroad through the Everglades with Barron Collier, a tycoon in his own right.

The railroad never appeared, but Vanderbilt returned the next month to announce the start of a tabloid newspaper along the lines of the two he ran in California. He advertised a $1,000 prize to the person who came up with the best name.

In the meantime, however, Vanderbilt managed to make himself vastly unpopular. Writing for his California papers, he panned the Florida climate and alleged that the waters off the beaches were full of sharks. Worse yet, he insinuated that land prices were "inflated." When the Miami *Herald* reprinted his musings, Vanderbilt backed down, muttering something about having had a bad cold and not really feeling himself. Vanderbilt did, however, launch the *Illustrated Daily Tab* on January 12, 1925. The tabloid died with the boom in 1926. Another newspaper launched in 1924, the *Tribune,* met the same fate.

As 1925 rolled in, realty left reality. Winter in Florida brought a huge crowd, some coming for the sun but many also coming because of the fabled promise of Florida real estate. The big rise in prices in 1924 hadn't gone unnoticed, primarily because developers and real estate hucksters hadn't limited their ads to the Miami *Herald.* Across the country, developers were using superlatives usually reserved for religious experiences to describe south Florida. The advertising began mostly in small papers in the Midwest, telling readers that Florida was the as-yet unappreciated playground of America. Other developers tried ploys like offering free trips to Miami to lure prospects.

But the biggest lures in Florida fever were the continuing rise in land prices and the whispers of huge fortunes made with little money down. Once again, the great lure of real estate came to the fore: leverage. If you put 10 percent down—the usual requirement—you could double your money with a 10 percent rise in prices. And in Florida in the early days of 1925, stories of those sorts of gains were easy to come by. Real estate was selling at tremendous prices. Old Fort Dallas fetched $500,000; the future mayor of Miami Beach sold his house for $150,000. He'd paid $800 for it 11 years earlier. A wheeler-dealer interviewed in the February 1925 issue of *Liberty* magazine claimed to have turned two quarts of bootlegged gin into $75,000 in eight months.

Into this growing atmosphere of speculation stepped the "binder boys," real estate agents who dealt in the raw stuff of real estate speculation: purchase and sale agreements, or binders. Normally, one would expect that the tedious pace of real estate deals would slow down any land boom; in Florida, however, they'd found a way to circumvent that. Here's how it worked:

By signing a binder, you'd become nominal holder of the land and obligated to pay the mortgage. You'd fork over your 10 percent of the purchase price—plus commission—to the real estate agent and would be obligated to pay the first installment of the mortgage 30 days later. In general, you'd be expected to pay off the entire mortgage within two or three years, 30-year mortgages being just a gleam in a mortgage lender's eyes in those days.

Becoming the owner of the property, however, also allowed you to sell it. When you entered the binder market, however, you didn't intend to make that first mortgage payment. You expected to resell the property, often within days, to someone else, who would sign yet another binder. The process, theoretically, could go on forever, at least as long as you could find a buyer. The binder boys played the "bigger fool" game: It doesn't matter what you buy or what price you paid for it as long as a bigger fool comes by willing to pay a bigger price for it.

The binder boys quickly became a fixture in Miami, and, for that matter, any town of any importance in Florida. Kenneth Ballinger, in *Miami Millions,* the only book to my knowledge on the Florida land boom, describes them like this:

> A composite picture of the binder boy possibly would reveal an individual slightly under normal height, never very clean or neat, bending every effort to making a lot of money in a hurry without the slightest pretense of remaining in Florida once that was done. He was attired in golf knickers, because they didn't need pressing or the addition of a coat, and the binder boy made the knicker at one time standard male daylight garb in almost every gathering, even church.

He spoke in a peculiar dialect, which soon had the natives pronouncing "binder" to rhyme with "cinder" instead of "kinder." He slept in hotel or rooming house halls, three and four to a single room, or wherever he could find temporary space.

The binder boys would accost passers-by with a variety of pitches, ranging from the hard sell—"The only man who hasn't made money in Florida real estate is the one who doesn't own any"—to a simple "Any lots today?" Weather permitting, they haunted the streets near the railroad station, or any other busy street for that matter, armed with books of binders and blueprints of lots.

Throughout the winter of 1925, construction continued apace, with announcements for new hotels, racetracks, civic centers, developments, and casinos, some of which were actually built. As the winter crowd lolled about the beaches and toured the area, however, one thing became abundantly apparent: South Florida needed numerous civic improvements. Miami's traffic in 1924 was a mess, primarily because the Florida East Coast Railroad used Flagler Street, one of the city's main avenues, as a switching point for its trains. The road was closed because of train traffic more often than it was open. In addition, the one causeway to Miami Beach, built in 1912, was clearly inadequate. Several more were planned. Not only that, but Miami needed other improvements, including wider roads, new roads, more railways, airports, water lines, sewage lines, and electric utilities.

Many of the towns, flush with money from building permits and tax income from new arrivals, went about improving themselves the old-fashioned way: by borrowing money in the municipal bond market. Muni bonds are beloved by the rich because their interest payments are free from federal and, in some cases, state taxes. Cities, towns, and states love them since a muni, being tax-free, allows municipalities to borrow at lower rates of interest than if they went to a bank. So Miami, along with Coral Gables and other communities, went happily into hock to improve the municipality.

As winter turned to spring in 1925, it was clear that "Florida fever" was rising. One sign was that there were more visitors in April than there were in January. And the visitors, lured by more and more advertising and more and more rumors of fabulous fortunes to be made, wanted land.

Developers were happy to accommodate. Silver Crest, a development opened in April, sold out in 10 minutes. East Shenandoah sold $3 million in lots in two days. Boca Raton sold $2.2 million in one day.

As you might expect, the real estate brokerage industry puffed up like a bullfrog in mating season. By the summer of 1925, 2,000 real estate offices and 25,000 real estate agents were plying their trade up and down the Florida coast. In July, Miami alone accredited nearly 6,000 brokers and continued to do so at the rate of 60 a day. The binder boys became so brazen that it was impossible to walk down the street without being accosted by a man in a straw hat with a blueprint in his hand. Miami, later that summer, would have to pass an ordinance forbidding buying and selling real estate on busy streets. Buses and cars brought "prospects" out to view raw swampland that would someday be dotted with millionaires' houses and yachts.

To real estate agents, the glass is never half empty: it's full. So "inside lots" were often miles from Miami, usually to the west near the Tamiami Trail, a planned road that was closer to a trail than a road. As is usual when real estate gets out of control, outlying areas saw prices rise, too, and some of the outlying areas existed only in the minds of the people who sold lots there. Inside or outside, some lots sold as many as eight times a day, each time for a higher price. The Florida East Coast Air Line, a local railroad, saw its stock price rise as investors, under the impression it was an airline, bid heavily for its stock.

As summer came to Florida, the developers' advertising and the rumors of huge profits in Florida land came to a head. If you can imagine what Woodstock would have been like if it were run by real estate agents, you can imagine Florida in the summer of 1925. Gertrude Matthews Shelby, a journalist assigned to cover the boom for *Harper's,* described it this way:

> "Let's drive down this summer when it's quiet," said canny people to one another in whispers, "and pick up some land cheap." . . . Once there, they found themselves in the midst of the mightiest and swiftest popular migration in history. . . . From everywhere came the land-seekers, the profit-seekers. Automobiles moved across the eighteen-foot-wide Dixie highway, the main artery of East Coast traffic, in a dense, struggling stream. Immense buses bearing subdivision names rumbled down loaded with "prospects" from Mobile, Atlanta, Columbia or from the northern steamers discharging at Jacksonville. . . . Most of the cars brimmed over with mother, father, grandmother, several children, and the dog, enticed by three years of insidious publicity about the miracles of Florida land values.

Shelby, it should be noted, wasn't entirely able to keep her journalistic distance from the event. She bought a lot in Miami and claimed a $13,000 profit.

The summer visitors clearly weren't there for the joys of a Florida summer. Farming was now at a standstill, and fresh vegetables commanded premium prices. No building materials were allowed to be shipped into Florida; all available train space was limited to passengers and food. Even bottled drinks and chewing gum were embargoed in late summer.

Hotels were packed to the closets with guests, and many of Miami's visitors had to sleep in the train station or out in the open. Blackouts were common, as the state's utilities struggled to keep up with the summer crowd, which, by now, had doubled the city's population. The water supply was brackish and often inadequate.

Also characteristic of that Florida summer were the ice famines. We don't think of ice as a particularly big commodity these days since it's easy enough to grab some from the freezer. As you may be aware from the tales of your parents or grandparents, however, the ice chests of the 1920s were just that: a lower compartment where you kept food and an upper compartment where you put the ice, which was delivered by the ice man. The new population quickly wore out Miami's ice stocks, and ice was severely rationed—to the point where the only way to get ice was by prescription.

Nevertheless, the boom roared merrily along. One broker advised Shelby, "The people who have made real fortunes checked their brains before leaving home. Buy anywhere. You can't lose." Another said, "All Florida is good. What you are really buying at the bottom is the bottom of the climate. Or the Gulf Stream. All you've got to do is *Get the rich consciousness.*"

As the crowds stayed—and bought—that halcyon summer, a few signs boded ill for the market. For one thing, the Internal Revenue Service announced that it would be looking into some of the fabulous gains claimed by real estate wheeler-dealers. Specifically, it would be looking into getting its share of some of the gains claimed.

The only problem, of course, is that although precious few real estate deals are made for cash, the IRS usually doesn't take an IOU. Most of the profits made in Florida real estate were on paper, and the paper they were written on was mighty thin. A man who made a $50,000 profit on a lot, for example, didn't usually get $50,000 in bat hides on the barrelhead; he got a portion of the downpayment and a promissory note to be paid as the mortgage money came in. What's more, the person who owed the $50,000 had probably already sold the lot again and was waiting for Bigger Fool C to resell the land to Bigger Fool D.

So the arrival of the IRS put some selling pressure on the Florida real estate market. By late August of 1925, another ill omen appeared: The binder boys, once a common sight, had begun to leave Miami. Many of them were broke. A good number of them came to financial grief in August, at the sale of a development called Seminole Beach. Although rumor was rife that the binder boys were the victims of a plot by developers, the truth is probably that the bigger-fool theory had run its course: There just weren't enough bigger fools around for the binder boys to make a profit. A great many of the binder boys leaped onto the first offering of lots at Seminole Beach but were unable to resell them quickly enough to get away from the first mortgage payment. As a result, many left hurriedly.

Although few knew it at the time, the summer of 1925 marked the high point of the boom. Building permits peaked that October, as did bank loans. As September drew on, Florida promoters began to sound defensive: The boom wasn't over, it was just taking a healthy breathing space. Many even argued that there had been no boom at all: Instead, Florida land prices were simply making up for the long decades when prices hadn't budged.

Meanwhile, developers brought out their big guns in advertising. Coral Gables, which was now the premier development of the boom, imported William Jennings Bryan, "the Boy Orator of the Platte," whose speeches at the turn of the century had won him nationwide admiration and whose role in the Scopes monkey trial was to bring him further notoriety. Bryan had long been a resident of Miami and dabbled in real estate himself. In a sad comedown for his oratory skills, he was hired for $100,000 —half to be paid in lots—to stand on a platform above a lagoon, pitching the wonders of Florida real estate. His follow-up act was a scantily clad dancer.

Nevertheless, the bloom was off the Florida rose. Those who had bought in the summer retired to watch their investments grow; the winter crowd in 1926 was smaller than the 1925 summer crowd and smaller even than the winter crowd in 1925. Development in 1926 was about a third of what it had been the previous year. In 1925, 971 new subdevelopments sprang into being in Dade county. In 1926, the number plunged to 395. The Miami *Herald's* ad lines peaked in January 1926.

Real estate booms normally don't end dramatically: In the usual course of events, you simply start to notice that there are more "for sale" notices in the newspaper, and that your jerk of a neighbor isn't bragging about the value of his house as much as he used to. At first, that was what happened in Florida.

The stories that filtered back from Florida in the spring and summer of 1926 were not of spectacular successes but of astounding losses. The binder trade, bereft of the binder boys, began to dwindle—to the point where the number of mortgage defaults began to rise steadily. The result was a legal nightmare. Trade in binders had been so brisk, with turnover so frequent, that finding the real owner of a piece of property was like trying to decide who really owns sections of the Middle East. Many of the titles issued in the summer of 1925 were not filed, and many of those that were weren't filed properly. In some cases, farmers who had kicked themselves for selling choice acreage for $17 an acre found themselves once again in possession of that land, because none of the dozens of subsequent sales stood up to legal snuff.

As speculators defaulted on their mortgages, banks began to fail as well. By 1928, far fewer banks graced the Miami area than had done so in 1925. Bank deposits fell to half the size of what they'd been during the crest of the Florida speculation. By 1932, when the effects of the Great Depression were factored into the equation, only two banks remained in Dade county.

The banks weren't the only ones to suffer. The communities that had borrowed for improvements during the boom soon found themselves short of the cash needed to service their debts. The decrease in sales led to a decrease in building permits. Since Florida then, as now, had no income taxes, the increase in population didn't translate directly into an increase in state revenues. By the end of the decade, Miami, Miami Beach, Coral Gables, and a host of other communities would default on their bonds.

Any thoughts of a resurgence of Florida land activity died forever in September 1926, when a hurricane devastated the Miami area. Frederick Lewis Allen, in *Only Yesterday,* describes it this way:

> Hitting the Gold Coast early in the morning of September 18, 1926, it piled the waters of Biscayne Bay into the lovely Venetian developments, deposited a five-masted steel schooner high in the street at Coral Gables, tossed big steam yachts upon the avenues of Miami, picked up trees, lumber, pipes, tiles, debris, and even small automobiles and sent them crashing into the houses, ripped the roofs off thousands of jerry-built cottages and villas, almost wiped out the town of Moore Haven on Lake Okeechobee, and left behind it some 400 dead, 63 injured, and 50,000 homeless.

When the storm clouds had cleared, the boom was gone with it. By 1927, most of the storm damage had been cleaned up, but the damage from the boom would litter the landscape for at least a decade. Real estate brokers shut down their offices, and Miami suffered a glut of office space well into the 1930s. A dozen or so hotels stopped in mid-construction and were not finished until half a decade after the worst of the Great Depression was over. Many more remained as blueprints. All over Florida, half-finished, or actually half-started, developments studded the landscape; unpaved roads, dotted with unconnected streetlamps, led into Florida swampland. Many developments were simply lands cleared of productive fruit trees, the only sign of development being a gateway with a ridiculous name over the entrance.

MR. PONZI GOES
TO FLORIDA

Charles Ponzi and Florida were a match made in heaven.[1]

Ponzi[2] was born in Italy and immigrated to Canada early on.[3] He began his career nobly helping his fellow Italian immigrants convert Canadian dollars into Italian lira to send back to the homeland. Ponzi even mailed the checks for the newly arrived North Americans.[4]

Ponzi soon soured of Canada, with its long winters, poor prospects, and unaccountably harsh view towards kiting checks.[5] He set his sights on Boston, with its long winters and vast reserves of unsuspecting Italian immigrants.[6]

---

[1]If your idea of heaven is selling swampland.

[2]Also known as Charles Bianchi and Charles Ponsi.

[3]From Italy's point of view, the earlier the better.

[4]Inexplicably, many of them never arrived in Italy, due, no doubt, to the slovenly Italian mail service.

[5]Canadian prisons have come a long way since then.

[6]Ponzi always had a fondness for his fellow countrymen.

Ponzi tried his hand at a variety of jobs, none of them successfully.[7] As a last resort, he started a pyramid scam of epic proportions.[8]

Ponzi's scheme has become a byword in white-collar crime. On the surface, it was a mildly plausible scheme whereby he traded international postal reply coupons in order to profit from currency differences.[9]

Underneath, it was—well, a Ponzi scheme.[10] Ponzi promised investors a 40 percent return in 90 days. Investors rose to the bait, and some even made money.[11]

Encouraged by his success, he later upped the ante to 50 percent in 90 days, then 100 percent.[12] Needless to say, he became wildly popular—and wealthy. At the height of his fortune, he liked to carry a gold-tipped cigarette holder and ride about in a cream-colored Locomobile.[13]

You can see the problem with this, of course. Eventually, everyone would have become rich, and then no one would have needed Ponzi.[14] Several newspapers pointed out that there weren't enough international postal reply coupons to make all that much money, and soon the district attorney got into the act as well.

---

[7]Probably because they were all legitimate.

[8]A man's got to make a living, after all.

[9]Plausible, that is, if you've never heard of international postal reply coupons. There were just never enough of them around to make a whole lot of money on.

[10]His company was named the Securities and Exchange Company—a nice touch.

[11]He paid them with other investors' money.

[12]And why not?

[13]Locomobiles were big in some circles.

[14]Life is full of little problems like this.

Things went from bad to worse. Upon investigation, the D.A. found out that he'd only bought $30 worth of postal coupons, against which he'd taken in $3 million.[15] Ponzi served three years in the slammer, was released on parole, and arrested again.

In 1926, vowing to make good to all his burned investors, Ponzi was released on bail. He headed to Florida and formed the Carpon Investment Company.

Seeing the demand for Florida land, Ponzi decided to do a little subdeveloping.[16] In his inimitable style, he promised investors 200 percent profit in 60 days. Unfortunately, the plan didn't materialize.[17]

Ponzi then headed off to jail for another term. When he was released, he was deported to Italy. After another fling at legitimate work, he was laid off. At the end of World War II, he left for the greener pastures of Brazil. There he died in a charity ward—a fitting end for one who had always relied on the kindnesses of strangers.

AFTERWORD

Even today, the Florida real estate market has never quite escaped its reputation for speculation and fraud. In 1989, for example, Miami-based developer General Development Corporation went into bankruptcy, leaving some 11,000 investors in the lurch.

---

[15]Leverage is indeed a wonderful thing.
[16]He was very good at it. He got 23 lots to the acre.
[17]He was arrested.

The case hasn't been resolved at this writing, but those who invested in the company allege that Florida land investors would have been right at home with GDC. Investors who bought lots or houses from GDC say they would get frequent phone calls from salesmen telling them how much they'd made—and urging them to buy more before lot prices went through the roof.

The lots weren't under water, but those who eventually settled in the lots they'd bought found out two distressing facts: First of all, in most cases, the land was worth far less than they'd been led to believe. One investor, told that his large home and swimming pool was worth $216,000, found out the property was worth just $92,000 when he went to refinance his mortgage. Other investors say that GDC's usual response to those who discovered the extent to which their land was overvalued was foreclosure.

Those who did settle down for the long term discovered that little, if any, planning went into the communities. The development town of Port St. Lucie, for example, has a population of 60,000, with only two major roads—each with two lanes. There's little room for parks or schools. Just lots.

All of which goes to prove, of course, that a determined sales force can sell just about anything. Unlike the 1920's boom, the GDC fiasco wasn't a mass movement; it apparently was just a sales job that went better than expected—much to the distress of its investors. One can only suspect, however, that the GDC affair is just a part of the land boom that was a hallmark of the 1980s, starting with Texas real estate and later migrating north to New England. Whether the 1980's land rush will end as badly as the one in Florida in 1920 or the one across the country in 1836 is anyone's guess. Given the long, slow recovery from both periods, one can only hope not.

Although most people have heard "Florida swamp-land" in concert with frauds, relatively little has been written about it. In retrospect, it looks somewhat like a passing fancy in the annals of financial foolishness. In reality, it was actually a prelude to the fiascos that followed in 1929.

SELECTED BIBLIOGRAPHY

Allen, Frederic Lewis. *Only Yesterday*. New York: Harper & Row, 1931. Probably the best book written on the 1920s. The chapter on Florida is priceless.

Ballinger, Kenneth. *Miami Millions*. Miami, Fla.: The Franklin Press, Inc., 1936. The only book, to my knowledge, that explores the Miami land boom extensively—and a wonderful portrait of life in Southern Florida in the 1920s.

Galbraith, John Kenneth. *The Great Crash 1929*. Boston: Houghton Mifflin Co., 1954. One of the best—and most readable—books on the Crash. His arch comments on the Florida boom shouldn't be missed.

CHAPTER 5

MUTUAL MISHAPS

In January of 1990, the mutual-fund industry passed a milestone: The total assets of the nearly 3,000 funds registered in the United States passed $1 trillion. It is a figure that lends itself to the sort of statistics that successful industries like to trot out on such occasions. One household in four, for instance, now owns mutual-fund shares. More stock market mutual funds are available to the investor than are stocks on the American Stock Exchange. The funds' assets under management are roughly enough to run the United States government for one year or to equal the entire gross national product of Haiti for the next 7,000 years.

Needless to say, mutual funds are popular investments—and with good reason. Most people don't have the time or experience to build a portfolio of common stocks, much less bonds or money market instruments. Those who do are probably such hopeless nerds that you wouldn't want to know them. What's more, most regular folks don't have the cash on hand to play the market the way the big players do—in hundred-share "round lots" in the case of the stock market or in $100,000 minimum denominations in the case of the money markets.

The funds have worked hard to get all that money, and few would hesitate to recommend them. Nevertheless, the funds had a long, uphill battle to convince people that they were worthy of the public trust. The reason for this had nothing to do with the inherent financial stodginess of the populace. It had to do with the fact that the fund industry, in its exuberant youth, burned the American public badly. The old-time funds—they're considerably different now and highly regulated to boot—were so bad, in fact, that someone who had invested over the course of the years from July 1927 to the end of 1937 could expect to be paid about 5 cents on the dollar, while an investment in the Standard & Poor's index of 500 common stocks would have been worth about 48 cents on the dollar. Here's the story of the funds that the mutual-fund industry would like to forget.

People have probably toyed with the idea of mutual funds ever since the first cave man was turned away from a sneering financial institution: "We're sorry, Mr.—Oop, was it?—but the minimum account here is 50 oxen. First Agricultural, down the street, might accept a goat, but I really wouldn't know." The idea behind a fund is relatively simple: Fred might not have enough money to buy, say, a $10,000 Treasury bill, but if Tom, Dick, and Harry chip in, all four could buy the bill and get a proportionate amount of the proceeds. Carried further, a group of investors could buy several issues of common stocks and get the advantage of diversification: If one their holdings went down that long, lonesome road to Chapter 11, the profits from the rest of the portfolio would cushion the loss.

The idea of pooled cash had been attempted in banking with relatively good success. Savings and loan associations, which now seem to be assigned to the scrap heap of financial history, were, in a way, a variant of the mutual-fund concept. With the exception of those that have converted to stock ownership, most depositors in savings associations are shareholders with the right to vote in the institution's annual meetings. The purpose of the association was to raise funds cheaply, through their members' deposits, in order to lend to members cheaply at low interest. The associations were also supposed to encourage thrift in their members, which is why you'll often see an S&L referred to as a "thrift." By and large, it should be noted, those S&Ls that stuck to their knitting and their original purposes have survived the current S&L crisis.

The concept of a mutual investment company—a company whose sole purpose was to invest in the stocks and bonds of other companies—goes back to the 1870s in England. During that period, and for the next 30 years or so, English bonds yielded, on average, about 3 percent. American bonds, on the other hand, yielded about 6 percent. Naturally, this was enough to make most English investors' heads turn. In particular, it caught the eye of one Robert Fleming, a bookkeeper at the English textile firm of Edward Baxter & Son. Fleming formed an investment association in 1873 and proposed to put the proceeds into a variety of American railroad bonds. The trust performed well, and the idea caught on in England, reaching a peak of sorts in 1890, when about 16 trusts were formed

The English trusts picked a bad time to rise to popularity, however. In 1890, Argentina hit one of its many economic air pockets and quickly slid into depression. This was unfortunate, not only for the Argentineans, but for the English trust managers as well, who had discovered that Argentine bonds paid even higher interest rates than their U.S. cousins. One brokerage house, Baring Brothers & Co., was particularly keen on Argentine bonds, and its investment trusts were packed full of them. So were most of the other English investment trusts at the time, many of which went spectacularly broke along with the Baring Brothers that year. The Baring affair considerably dampened English enthusiasm for investment trusts until shortly before the First World War.

Meanwhile, in America, the idea of an investment trust was slowly taking hold. U.S. investors weren't impressed with the performance of the English trusts and, by and large, stayed away from the idea until about the turn of century. An early version of the mutual fund appeared in 1904 in Maine, of all places, in the form of the Railway Light and Securities Company.

Like all of the early mutual funds, Railway was a closed-end mutual fund, a term that deserves some explanation. Closed-end funds aren't the same sort that you see these days advertising for your cash in every major financial periodical; those are open-ended funds, and we'll get around to them presently. A closed-end fund is a company just like U.S. Steel or North American Hat Blocking; the closed-end fund's primary line of business, however, is buying and selling securities, such as stocks or bonds. As with any company whose shares trade openly, a closed-end fund raises its capital by selling its shares to the public. The company pays off the underwriter of the issue, who arranges the legal niceties of the stock offering as well as the sales of the shares. The closed-end fund then pockets the remaining proceeds and invests them in whatever its charter allows. Like any other company, a closed-end fund can raise or lower its dividend at will, or authorize stock splits.

The funds grew slowly in popularity until 1927, when the public began to take a shine to them in a big way. The main reason for the funds' popularity was relatively simple. Starting in 1927 and continuing until 1929, the stock market did remarkably well, at least until the bull market made its rendezvous with destiny on Black Tuesday and Black Thursday in October 1929. During the bull market, with the market making new records regularly, the funds virtually sold themselves.

The funds had two big selling points. First of all, when you buy a fund, you get a lot more bang for your buck than you do with a single stock. If you spend $100 on Acme Toaster, that's all you get. However, $100 in the Bullmoose Fund gives you a bit of General Electric, a bit of Standard Oil, a bit of Steel, and a bit of some tiny stocks that are known to but a few.

The funds' second selling point was that they were run by movers and shakers in the stock market, men who not only knew how to play the market, but probably had some pretty strong inside information as well. The public widely believed that the biggest players did more than just look at a company's earnings and the prospects for the economy as a whole. The really big movers could "take a stock in hand" and, through aggressive buying, send its price soaring.

The public's belief was well-founded. Although officially discouraged, bull and bear pools did operate in the markets of the 1920s, much as they did in the previous century when Daniel Drew, Cornelius Vanderbilt, Jim Fiske, and Jay Gould plundered their way through the securities markets in the 1860s. In the 1920s, the big operators were such people as William Crapo Durant, the Fischer brothers, and Jesse Livermore, who have been credited with orchestrating many of the big moves on the Big Board during the bull market. Supposedly, they drove RCA from a $40 stock to over $500 per share. The men who ran the funds—inside men, with years of experience on Wall Street—surely knew the big operators and knew more than a few secrets as well, the public believed.

If this belief sounds wonderfully quaint to you, it's one that lingers to this day, despite the zealous eyes of the Securities and Exchange Commission. Although the focus has shifted from people who actively (if unethically) manipulate stocks, every week brings breathless interviews with Wall Street pros, ranging from brokerage house analysts to mutual-fund managers to private investors. The cult of the "smart money" lives on.

At any rate, the fund industry grew at a rate that even the ebullient Dow Jones Industrial Average couldn't match. The numbers for the industry are the sort that make statisticians' eyes water. In 1927, for example, the funds had annual sales of $400 million; by 1929, the funds had sold $3 billion. That's a 650 percent increase, or a 186.6 percent annual growth rate. To put that into some perspective, consider the case of a baby girl whose weight was 8 pounds at birth. The girl would weigh 52 pounds on her third birthday and 181 pounds on her fifth birthday. By the time she'd reached her 18th year, she'd weigh 300 tons and qualify for statehood.

Other statistics on the mutual-fund industry were equally impressive. In 1928, for example, the investment trusts had 55,000 shareholders; by 1929, they had 525,000. That's roughly a 900 percent increase in two years. At that rate, the 8-pound baby girl would weigh 1,549,682 tons when she graduated high school and be eligible for membership in the Galactic Federation. As a Senate investigatory committee later noted, "A veritable epidemic of investment trusts afflicted the nation."

As assets and shareholders increased, so did the number of funds. On Wall Street, the reasoning is that if one product sells well, 20 similar ones should sell just as well. About 600 new funds appeared on the scene between 1927 and 1929. The pace was the quickest in 1929, when an average of a fund a day made its debut.

One reason that there were so many funds was that it was awfully easy to start one. The United Founders Group, for example, which eventually became a network of some 13 different funds, started out with $500 in borrowed cash. An employee of the First Income Trading Corporation, under Congressional examination, described the offices this way:

Q. Where were the offices of First Income?

A. 25 Broadway.

Q. The same place where the Trans-Atlantic (another mutual fund) office was?

A. Yes.

Q. In the same room?

A. Yes, sir.

Q. How many desks did you have there?

A. Well, they had three desks there.

First Income was somewhat more affluent than another major investment company, the Eastern Utilities Trading Corporation, which had no offices, clerical staff, or management of its own. The fund was a subsidiary of Associated Gas and Electric, a major East Coast utility company. The Congressional inquiry into Eastern Utility's operations must have been enlightening to its shareholders:

Q. You think there may have been one man who devoted all of his time to Eastern Utilities Investment Company affairs?

A. I think there may have been.

Q. Are you sure of that?

A. No.

The funds were not only easy to set up, they were immensely profitable to their sponsors. There were, of course, the usual perks of running a multimillion-dollar fund. First of all, being in command of a fund then, as now, meant that you could curry favor with brokers who were anxious to transact your trades. Secondly, you could collect management fees—generally a percentage of the fund's assets—in return for running the fund.

There were other benefits, too, though not quite as straightforward. An investment banker, speaking at a convention in 1928, described a run-in he'd had with a man from a brokerage house who had come to New York to start a fund. The banker asked why he was so keen on starting a fund. "My firm has been entirely dependent on other people's securities," the man told the banker. "We have not been able to get anybody else's securities, so one reason I want to form an investment trust is to manufacture securities to sell."

The funds were not only a way to manufacture securities, but a place to put manufactured securities as well. For example, the funds could absorb large amounts of stock that its sponsor had for sale but couldn't sell successfully to the public. If the fund were the major buyer of a stock, it could drive up the price of the stock considerably, tending to pique the public's interest in the remaining stock. The practice also ran up the value of the fund's portfolio, which went a long way toward drumming up interest in the fund. This type of "dumping" was relatively common among the funds.

As more funds arrived on the scene, they became as varied as insects in a tropical rain forest. Some, such as the Public Utility Holding Corporation of America, concentrated on a particular sector of the stock market that was currently in favor. Utilities stocks were one of the biggest hits of the 1920s, unlike today, when they're considered one step above bank deposits as investments. At the time, however, utilities were merrily buying, selling, and expanding and were considered a major growth industry of the time. (Keep in mind that electricity wasn't an amenity in all homes at that time.) Other big favorites were chain stores, tobacco, and, of course, that all-American favorite, technology.

Other funds, such as the Central States Electric Corporation, purported to concentrate on one market sector in one particular region. These highly specialized companies were legion: According to one estimate, 25 percent of the funds in 1936 specialized in one industry. The problem with specialized funds, of course, is that while they're fine when the industry is hot, they tend to stink up the place when the industry grows cold. In most cases, specialized funds eventually bore witness to Darwin's dictum that specialization leads to extinction.

Yet others rode the coattails of the big investment houses. Some of the highest fliers were the Goldman Sachs Trading Corporation, sponsored by the tony investment house of Goldman, Sachs & Company, and the Lehman Corporation, founded by Lehman Brothers. These funds had wide-ranging investment charters. They could—and did—invest in nearly anything.

Most of the companies had one thing in common: They could make liberal use of margin, or borrowed money, for buying stocks or selling them short. By doing so, you can make more money when the market is with you. You can also lose your shirt if the market is against you. In those more robust days of the stock market, you could put 10 percent or less down on your stock purchase and borrow the rest from your broker. As in the case of any transaction that involves leverage, or borrowed money, the effects on your holdings can be electrifying: A 10 percent rise in price can double your investment, and a 10 percent fall can wipe you out.

Some funds used margin quite well. The Railway Fund, for example, survived the crash, converted to an open-ended fund, and changed its name to The Colonial Fund, Inc., which is open for business today at its Boston headquarters and doing nicely. (Like most modern funds, it no longer uses margin.) Other funds that used margin, however, didn't fare so well.

One reason was the 1929 market crash and subsequent bear market, which took the Dow Jones Industrial Average from a 1929 high of 383 to a 1932 low of 41. That's a loss of 89 percent, the largest since the panic and depression of 1836. Those who were on margin during that period, it can be assumed, took a considerably larger drubbing than those who paid the full price in cash.

Had the use of margin been the only problem with mutual funds at the time, the industry probably wouldn't have had to endure all those nasty government hearings from 1937 to 1940, nor would the Investment Company Act of 1940 have been necessary. The industry came up with a number of innovations, however, that were later to become interesting case studies in how securities industry practices become outlawed.

In the heady days of the late 1920s, the only question seemed to be how to make the most of a perpetually rising market. To the mutual-fund industry, the answer was simple: If a leveraged mutual fund could amplify stock market gains, why not create a mutual fund that invested only in mutual funds? And since leverage worked for the funds that the fund of funds was investing in, why not use borrowed cash for the purchases of the fund of funds as well?

This is the kind of reasoning that gets people to do really stupid things. It's a bit like saying that if driving at 60 miles per hour is good, then driving at 120 miles per hour is twice as good. Nevertheless, the fund-of-funds concept caught on quickly, and soon there were even third-tier funds—leveraged funds of funds that invested in leveraged funds of funds.

Being in a highly leveraged fund can be a wonderful thing when the stock market is on the way up—which it certainly was in 1928 and the bulk of 1929. Some of the funds racked up spectacular gains on the way up, but for the majority, the ride up was very brief. Since many of the funds—about 600, or half the industry—came into being in 1929, their share prices had nowhere to go but down when Wall Street walked off a cliff. The shares of the Public Utilities Holding Corporation of America, for instance, came out at about $36 per share, fell to $20 by the end of 1929, staggered up to $25 during the suckers' rally of 1930, and then swooned to under $1 per share by 1934.

The funds had another problem, which occurs to some extent with today's closed-end funds as well. The problem stemmed from the fact that people overpaid for their shares in the days of the roaring stock market. Here's why.

The exact value of a fund is fairly easy to calculate at the end of each business day. All you have to do is tally up the market value of each of the fund's holdings and divide by the number of shares outstanding. Suppose, for example, the Bullmoose Fund owned securities worth $1 million and that there were 100,000 shares outstanding. Each share, then, would be worth $100 if Bullmoose were to liquidate the portfolio and distribute its assets to its shareholder. Logic would dictate that Bullmoose would sell for $100 that day.

Logic, however, doesn't necessarily apply to the stock market. In most cases, closed-end funds sell for considerably more or less than value of the securities in the fund's portfolio. The reason is that the people who buy stocks aren't logical. If a fund manager has—or is rumored to have—a particularly hot hand, people will pay $110 for a fund worth $100 per share. The reason: Investors feel that paying the premium is worth it, considering the fund's prospects. Paying $110 for a fund worth $100 per share seems cheap if you think the fund will be worth $200 in the near future. Conversely, if the fund manager has been seen rolling in the gutter after an all-night jag with cleaning fluid, the fund could sell at a discount, since investors might feel his performance is impaired and that the fund will shortly be worth $20 per share.

All of which is a long way of getting to the point that most of the closed-end funds in the late 1920s sold for considerable premiums over their real values. Investors were willing to pay $1.50 for every $1.00 the fund actually had. Part of the reason, of course, was the nation's love affair with the stock market in the late 1920s. The other reason was because the funds were, after all, run by big, professional players who knew the market. The highest fliers commanded the biggest premiums. For the Goldman Sachs Trading Corporation, buyers were willing to pay $2 for every $1 the fund controlled. The Central States Electric Utilities Corporation got $3 for every $1 in assets.

As early as 1928, warning bells were ringing. The National Association of Securities Commissioners, the national organization of state securities watchdogs, issued a report in 1928 warning about the funds' abuses. One of the major abuses uncovered involved the contractual plan, whereby an investor signed a contract agreeing to pour money into a fund over a certain period of time. This in itself was not a terrible thing, even though the sales fees ran as high as 10 percent. Unfortunately, as the public's lust for mutual funds continued unabated, the contractual plan became an ideal vehicle for con men. The method was simple: Print up a prospectus and sign up a number of investors for, say $25 or more a month into a fictitious mutual fund. Since the funds were sold for long-term investors, it could be months or years before the victim discovered that the Emerald City Fund, for instance, was pure fiction.

The crash brought down the good with the bad. The events of October 1929 have been examined more fully elsewhere, and by abler writers. (One of the best sources is *The Great Crash*, by John Kenneth Galbraith.) Needless to say, however, after October 1929, investors were less willing to pay premiums for their funds. In fact, most of the funds promptly dropped to a discount after Black Tuesday and Black Thursday, and stayed there for the next decade. To this day, in fact, most closed-end funds still trade at a discount to their actual liquidation values.

At any rate, the funds, along with most everything else in the country, dropped like a rock during the worst part of the great 1929 to 1932 bear market. In 1932, Goldman Sachs Trading Corporation traded at 1 percent of its 1929 high price. The only standout was the Lehman Corporation, which managed to trade at 23 percent of its 1929 high—considerably better than the market averages. As a group, however, the funds sold at an average of 6 percent of their 1929 highs in 1932. Many of the funds simply went bust. By 1932, the funds' assets had fallen to $2 billion from their 1929 high of $8 billion.

The crash—and the subsequent Congressional hearings into stock market activities—brought some of the worst practices to light. Consider, for example, the case of the Iroquois Share Corporation, a closed-end fund that came into being in January 1929. The fund was organized by O'Brian, Potter & Stafford, a Buffalo, New York, brokerage and investment banking firm. The fund was designed for the depositors of O'Brian's bank customers.

The fund's investors were doomed from the outset. Under the terms of the offering, O'Brian, Potter & Stafford was offered options to buy 50,000 shares—half again as large as the offering—for less than the price the public paid at its initial price of $20 per share. If the management had exercised its options, shareholders would have found their holdings worth one-third less overnight.

The Iroquois management didn't have to exercise their options to squash their shareholders' profits, however. O'Brian, Potter & Stafford dealt extensively with the stocks and bonds of small local banks in the Buffalo area, most of which were unlisted on the New York Exchange and traded thinly, if at all, elsewhere. The firm had brought many of the stocks into the world, and, since they were good enough for O'Brian, Stafford & Potter, they were good enough for the Iroquois Share Corporation.

The crash did the rest. After October 1929, the small bank stocks the fund owned had fallen 50 percent. The few stocks that weren't backed by small upstate New York banks fell only 15 percent.

The crash also squeezed the fund's sponsor considerably, and, to raise cash, O'Brian, Potter & Stafford sold the fund an unfinished office building in Buffalo. The fund's management, O'Brian, Potter & Stafford. obligingly sold some of the fund's portfolio at fire-sale profits in order to buy the building.

O'Brian and company sold Iroquois to the Atlas Share Corporation 27 months after the fund was formed. All told, the sponsors milked the fund for about $650,000. Over the same period, its investors lost about 60 percent. And by the time of the sale, April 1931, the bear market still had a year to run.

Iroquois was just one fund, and a relatively small one at that. The more successful funds spawned other funds, all of which eventually went down in flames. One of the most remarkable fund groups of the time was the Founders Group. It was founded by one William Bull, a broker from Bridgeport, Connecticut, and Christopher Coombs, a Boston-based broker. The fund group started small, with some $500 in borrowed capital. Nevertheless, Bull and Coombs were able to get some first-rate investment advice, in the form of Dr. Leland Rex Robinson, one of the most distinguished economists of the day. The early funds in the Founders Group had elaborate restrictions as to the type of stocks and bonds it could buy, although it wasn't bound to disclose its holdings.

The fund group set a record of sorts, raising $686 million by 1929, some $500 million of that paid in by the public. That in itself is not so impressive as what Founders did with the money. The 13 funds invested heavily in each other—on margin, of course—and in companies affiliated with the group. By using leverage in ways that probably have never been equaled since, United Founders eventually controlled assets of more than $2 billion.

For investors, the ride up was more than impressive—it was astronomical. Less than $1,000 invested in the American Founders Common Stock Fund in 1925, for instance, would have become about $10,500 by the fund's peak in 1929. The ride down was absolutely appalling, however: By the stock market's bottom in 1932, the $10,500 that American Founders was worth at its peak was worth less than $25. Many of the other Founders funds went straight to zero.

One would think that after taking such a terrific drubbing in the funds, investors would have shied away from them. Unfortunately, one would be wrong. One reason is that few believed, even after the crash, that the end had come for the stock market. This should be amply clear from the fact that on Black Tuesday, when 16 million shares traded in one of the greatest panics in history, there was a buyer for every seller.

More than that, however, was the fact that the market rallied well into 1930 after the crash. Before the crash, the market previously had fallen steeply and had always recovered. Investors were taught that the best time to buy was after such a fall, and many investors were caught in the trap. Although the early-1930 rally was the best-known sucker's rally of the Great Bear Market, it should be noted that the stock market staged several such rallies all the way to the bottom in 1932.

As the crash brought many of the closed-end funds low, a new type of fund became popular: the open-ended fund. Although not entirely new—the first such fund, Massachusetts Investors Trust, opened its doors in 1924—it had several distinct advantages over the closed-end fund. The open-ended fund's major difference is that an investor can redeem shares at the fund's net asset value at any time. The fund's net asset value is the value of its portfolio divided by the number of shares outstanding. In short, open-ended funds have no premiums or discounts. You get your share of the pie any time you want it.

Once again, some of the earliest funds rode out the storm well. Massachusetts Investors Trust is still around today and has served its customers well. Many of the funds that followed, however, did not do quite as well.

The relatively honest structure of the open-ended funds prohibited some of the more outrageous shenannegans of the closed-end funds. Nevertheless, some of the open-ended funds managed to find ways that were somewhat less than ethical to wring cash from their investors.

Then, as now, funds were offered by two major types of distributors. The first kind was those whose primary line of business was managing money. For a money manager, funds offered several benefits. First of all, a fund could showcase the company's talents at making a buck. Instead of concatenating the records of several dozen individual investors and creating a track record, the management company could point to their mutual fund and say, "That is how we manage money."

Funds were also a matter of convenience for successful money managers. When people discover that you have a talent for making money, they beat a path to your door. And money managers hate turning away investors' cash. So rather than refer customers to, say, the Warbucks Capital Management Company down the street, a successful money management firm could roll up its smaller accounts into one rather large mutual fund.

By and large, the money managers served their investors well. The biggest offenders in the 1930s were the companies that farmed out the management to others and lived to sell fund shares. And sell they did.

Selling funds, then as now, was a lucrative business. For one thing, there was the sales charge, or load, that funds levied on their parishioners. Currently, the highest load a fund can charge is 8.5 percent of the investment, and many funds charge far less. In the early 1930s, the maximum was whatever the market could bear, and in many cases, that was about 10 percent.

To an extent, loads are a necessary evil. Most people buy their investments through brokers, and brokers have bills to pay and families to raise. What's a good deal for a broker, however, isn't necessarily a good deal for you. If you pay 10 percent of your investment to a broker, you start out 10 percent in the hole. And, because of the remorseless logic of mathematics, a 10 percent loss requires an 11 percent gain before you break even.

Funds distributors whose main purpose in life was selling shares quickly found out how important a high load was to selling their funds. A broker who could recommend a fund with a 5 percent load or a 10 percent load naturally chose the fund with the higher load.

The most popular method of selling funds was the contractual plan, whereby the investor agreed to invest a certain amount into the fund each month for a specified period. This was wildly popular with brokers and with funds for two reasons. First of all, to speed up the brokers' reward for selling the contract, the bulk of the first several installments went directly into the brokers' pockets. Secondly, it provided a relatively stable cash flow and cushioned any exodus from the fund. Contractual plans were wonderful for brokers and for funds, but if the investor suddenly needed funds, he or she would find that much of the investment greatly diminished.

Funds that depended on brokers also found that they couldn't be terribly fussy about those who sold their shares. Restricting brokers, although a noble practice, meant restricting sales. As a result, many contractual plans were sold by brokers who were less than honest with their customers about the nature of their investments. The desperation measures taken to sell shares were aggravated by the fact that all investments involving stocks were awfully difficult to sell in the wake of the Depression.

In addition the contractual plans, the funds embarked on advertising that would have made P. T. Barnum blush. Fund ads implied that they could make people rich without telling that they could make people considerably poorer, too. Radio ads extolled the virtues of fund investing and alleged that the only way to get as rich as, say, John D. Rockefeller or J. P. Morgan was to invest in mutual funds.

Finally, some of the open-ended funds fell into some of the more disreputable practices of their closed-end cousins. Fund managers sometimes bought pet stocks that had little or no market elsewhere; when the market declined precipitously, as it did in 1929 and again in 1937, they had to sell their good stocks to cover redemptions. The reason was simple: There wasn't any market for the bad stocks. This left those shareholders remaining in the fund with a portfolio of virtually worthless stocks.

Just as 1929 was the high-water mark for closed-end funds, 1937 was the high-water market for open-ended funds. One of the little-known bits of Wall Street lore is that the period from 1932 to 1937 was the third-greatest bull market in history, when the market rose from its Depression low of 41 on the Dow to over 150. All good things come to an end, however, and in 1937 the prevailing mood was gloom. The Depression seemed as if it might never end, and stock prices tumbled. As they did, the values of closed- and open-ended funds fell right along with them.

The cries of outraged mutual fund shareholders were large; and, fortunately, they were heard—particularly by the Securities and Exchange Commission, which held hearings from 1936 to 1939 on the subject of mutual funds in general. The upshot was the Investment Company Act of 1940, which put an end to many of the more dubious mutual-fund practices of the day. Loads were limited, selling practices sharply curtailed, and the investor was put, if not in the driving seat, at least in the passenger seat. To this day, despite the occasional mutual-fund mishap, the Investment Company Act of 1940 has kept the mutual-fund industry, with few exceptions, squeaky clean.

S.O.S. FOR I.O.S.

If Bernie Cornfeld was anything, it was sincere.[1]

Cornfeld began his career as a socialist, until he found there wasn't any money in it. So in 1954 he moved into mutual funds.[2]

Bernie found that he was a natural at selling funds and at lining up other salesmen to do the same. By 1960, he had a whole legion of them working worldwide, with the slogan, "Do you sincerely want to be rich?"[3]

If anyone sincerely wanted to be rich it was Bernie, and he soon figured out that the best way to do so was to own your own mutual fund. His first fund, the IIT Fund, was formed in Luxemborg in late 1960. The U.S. investment climate was not right for a fund based stateside.[4]

---

[1]So were Jim and Tammy Bakker.
[2]It seemed logical at the time.
[3]"Workers of the world, invest!" never caught on.
[4]The Securities and Exchange Commission was a big part of the problem.

The fund didn't fare terribly well, mainly because of its penchant for investing in nearly fictitious stocks owned by the fund's director.[5]

Bernie's main stroke of genius, however, was in his creation of a fund of funds—in other words, a mutual fund that invested solely in other mutual funds.[6] The fund was based in Canada, mainly because the SEC kept finding fault with its structure.[7]

The Fund of Funds was a great deal.[8] Like most of Cornfeld's funds, it was sold on a contractural basis, which meant that salesmen kept the first six months' or so investment. The Fund of Funds also collected sales charges from the other funds it poured money into and charged performance and management fees as well.[9]

Cornfeld's funds eventually grew to about $2.5 billion, with money pouring in from all over the world. Much of this money went into Bernie's pockets, and he used that cash to show the proletariat just how goddamned exciting being a member of the leisured class could be.[10]

By 1969, Bernie's empire was ready to go public, which it did, to the tune of $110 million. Unfortunately, the tune quickly went sour, partly because of the bear market of 1970.[11] Bernie's empire quickly started losing cash, and investors started heading for the exits.

---

[5]Everything would have been fine if the companies hadn't collapsed.

[6]This concept had been tried before in the 1920s and 1930s. It didn't work then, either.

[7]It was illegal, for one thing.

[8]For Bernie.

[9]"We're in the business of totally converting the proletariat to the leisured class painlessly . . . it's revolutionary and it's goddamned exciting."—Bernie Cornfeld.

[10]Many of those he demonstrated this to were unusually buxom.

[11]Greed, incompetence, and dishonesty also played a role.

As investors left, the fund managers had to sell, and, since most of the investments in their portfolios were sheer garbage with no regular market, they sold off most of the good holdings. This left those still in the fund with a wide assortment of trash.[12]

Cornfeld's stock fell so precipitously that he was ousted from the company. In order to get the funds back in order, they elected Robert Vesco to take over. It was the wrong move. Vesco, through a complicated series of maneuvers, pillaged the funds for about $1 billion and fled the country. He's still on the run.[13]

Bernie, however, got out while the getting was good. He's alive and well and probably looking for a few good investors.

AFTERWORD

The effects of the Crash—and the Great Depression that followed it—were seared on the nation's memory. Most of those memories, however, seem to have slowly started to fade. The generation that lived through the Depression kept an abhorrence of debt and speculation. Those whose parents lived through that period took a more moderate road: Debt, in the form of credit cards and mortgages, was all right, provided it was done in moderation.

Now, some 50 years after the Great Crash, the country is again becoming antidebt, but only after indulging in a

---

[12]"What I have done is apply socialist ideas about redistributing wealth in a free-enterprise context."

[13]If you want to earn your fortune, all you have to do is get past his bodyguards and drag him back to the States.

rather spectacular binge. It's somewhat sobering to keep in mind that the total debt in the country—personal, corporate and governmental—is close to its all-time peak, when measured as a percentage of the gross national product. Should the economy tumble again, it's unlikely the government would be able to raise enough cash to bail the country out, or that interest rates could fall enough to provide any real relief.

If there is a general downturn in the economy, it would be hard to blame the mutual-fund industry, which has conducted a remarkably aboveboard—and booming—business. Of course, the industry has also had fairly stern rules and diligent regulators to keep it that way. Even so, given the venom of some of the things written about the funds in the 1930s, it's remarkable the industry survived at all. Books with titles like *Mutual Funds: The Dirty Odor from Overseas* and *Investment Trusts Gone Wrong!* accused the industry of everything from bilking investors to ruining the American capitalist system.

Some of the allegations about the funds proved true, of course. One of the Securities and Exchange Commission's largest worries about the funds was that, in a sharp market break, allowing investors to cash out could simply worsen the situation. In 1987, that fear was partly realized. On Friday, October 16, it became apparent that a large-scale downturn was underway, and mutual-fund companies were deluged with sell orders from worried investors. To meet redemptions, many funds were forced to sell off their stock holdings on October 19—Black Monday, when the Dow Jones Industrial Average fell more than 500 points. To make matters worse, many funds had to sell their best, and therefore most saleable, stocks because the market for smaller stocks had simply evaporated. As a result, some funds saw considerable damage to their portfolios, more so even than the Dow.

By and large, however, most of the funds came out of the crash admirably, with their legions of service representatives working well into the night to settle accounts. Investors took losses, but everyone got their fair share of what was left, on the day they asked for it—and the funds can promise nothing else. At this point, while there are some truly terrible funds on the market, those funds are only terrible because of their managers' inability to pick stocks and not because of chicanery on the part of their promotors. For that, at least, we owe a debt of gratitude to the actions of Congress and the regulators in the 1940s.

SELECTED BIBLIOGRAPHY

Bullock, Thomas. *Investment Trusts and Investment Companies.* Washington, D.C.: 1939. A defender of the mutual funds, Bullock also provides some useful history of their origins.

Flynn, John Thomas. *Investment Trusts Gone Wrong!* New York: New Republic, Inc., 1930. An early critic of investment trusts vents his spleen.

Galbraith, John Kenneth. *The Great Crash 1929.* Boston: Houghton Mifflin Co., 1954. Galbraith explores the role of Goldman, Sachs & Co. in the mutual fund industry in great—and acidic—depth.

National Association of Securities Administrators. Committee on Investment Trusts. *Report of the Committee on Investment Trusts of the National Association of Securities Commissioners, and Clippings from the President's Files.* St. Paul, Minn.: Author, 1929. In which state securities administrators, almost always in the vanguard of fraud detection, sound the first alarms.

U.S. Securities and Exchange Commission. *Investment Trusts and Investment Companies.* Washington, D.C.: U.S. Government Printing Office, 1939. The SEC. takes note.

United States Congress, Sentate Committee on Banking and Currency. *Investment Trusts and Investment Companies.* Washington, D.C.: U.S. Government Printing Office, 1940. Congress take large note—and is displeased with what it finds.

CHAPTER 6

SALAD DAYS FOR SALAD OIL

Every once in a while, two powerful forces come together and the result is catastrophe. In 1913, for example, the greatest ocean liner of its day, the Titanic, ran smack into one of nature's own ocean-bound behemoths, a nameless iceberg, and the Titanic came out the worse for it. In 1812, Napoleon Bonaparte, the greatest general of his day, ran into the Russian winter and was unable to defeat it. In 1963, a three-way catastrophe occurred when the American Express Company and the New York Stock Exchange met Anthony DeAngelis, the Salad Oil King of New Jersey and met one of the greatest embarassments in corporate history.

American Express is one of the most august names among blue-chip stocks. The company began its life in the 1850s, logically enough, as an express company. In those days, as now, express companies were designed to get packages from one place to another more quickly and more safely than normal. Nowadays, thanks to the wonders of commercial aircraft, a fast delivery is overnight or even the same day. Back then, when normal delivery time between New York and Buffalo could run a week or two, express companies took on a great importance, particularly considering the hazards along the way. Canalboats were slow, and didn't run in the winter; steamboats were somewhat faster, but didn't run in the winter, either. Stagecoaches were just as subject to the whims of the weather and were probably the most bone-jarring and uncomfortable means of transport known to man. Railroads were the best route, but didn't serve all cities, and the iron horses had alarming tendencies to run off the track, run into each other, or run out of steam. For someone with great stamina (and courage), the rewards of personally escorting packages by the fastest route possible could be substantial.

The biggest shippers of the time were banks, which needed to transfer gold, checks, and securities between one another in a safe and timely manner, which explains why the two biggest names in express companies then— American Express and Wells Fargo—are now also closely allied with the banking industry. Wells Fargo is a powerful bank in its own right, and American Express, through its credit cards and money orders, is a major financial institution today. The two companies were also closely allied with each other; Henry Wells and H. G. Fargo were two of the three founders of American Express. Wells and Fargo later split with American Express over the development of a new route to California.

By 1963, however, express delivery had become just a part of American Express. The company had become a multiline conglomerate, with its fingers in everything from lending to credit cards to field warehousing. It was the latter operation that got American Express into so much trouble.

American Express (Amex) began its field warehousing business in the 1940s, and it had the potential to be lucrative, although it never lived up to that potential, unfortunately for American Express. A field warehouse is not, as one might expect, where Farmer Bob keeps his winter wheat crop, although the business probably had its roots (as it were) in farming.

Instead, a field warehouse is a portion of a company plant that's used to store the collateral for a loan. Suppose, for example, you ran a bakery and went to your friendly neighborhood banker for a loan. "Certainly," your banker replies. "We're here to help you. We're the bank that works to earn your trust. What will you let us sieze and sell at auction if you go belly up before you repay your note?"

What your friendly banker is talking about here is collateral, and if he's a prudent banker, he'll ask for more collateral than the amount of the loan. After all, the price of wheat could fall, in which case he wouldn't recoup the full value of the note if your business was a half-baked venture. So you offer up 20 tons of wheat you have stored away. Now, your banker doesn't want you to dump 20 tons of wheat in the lobby, nor does he particularly want to rent out warehouse space to hold the wheat. In fact, he really doesn't want the wheat at all. He'd be much happier if he never had to deal with the wheat. But, on the other hand, he doesn't think a handshake is good enough security for the loan. So he sets up a field warehouse—a segregated spot on your property where he can check up on it from time to time.

Once the field warehouse is set up, you'll get a receipt for your wheat. The receipt is highly valuable since it becomes, in essence, proof of that you have the collateral for the loan. Because the collateral is so valuable, it's important that the warehouse is monitored closely and run strictly by the rules.

Like many things in banking, setting up and checking a field warehouse can be tedious. And some companies like to set up their field warehouses before they shop for a loan.

So companies sprang up to organize and monitor field warehouses. They would collect fees for the service and, in the meantime, establish good relationships with banks.

The fees were valuable to American Express, but having good relationships with banks were even more so. American Express was not a bank, but because of its credit card operations as well as its international travel and express divisions, it was frequently in the position of having to extend credit. And while the company's resources were considerable, being able to tap credit from banks was essential.

American Express Field Warehousing was never terribly profitable, however, and thus never merited much attention from the Amex top brass. The company remained a sleepy backwater from its inception through the 1950s—until, that is, Anthony DeAngelis came along.

DeAngelis came from a checkered background, to say the least. In 1953, as a head of Adolph Gobel, Inc., a wholesale meat and lard dealer, "Tino," as he was known, filed for reorganization under the bankruptcy laws. The reorganization was completed five years later. In 1958, he was indicted by a grand jury on charges of influencing a witness in a Securities and Exchange Commission case to give false testimony. He was acquitted. Tino had also run into some misunderstandings with the Internal Revenue Service along the way. He was, to put it mildly, not a great credit risk.

By the end of the 1950s, though, Tino was a Big Man in Bayonne. He controlled Allied Crude Vegetable Oil Refining Corporation as well as Freezer House Corporation, both of which were in sore need of field warehousing operations. The reason, of course, was that DeAngelis was who he was, and most lenders preferred to deal with him on a secured basis.

Fortunately, Tino had plenty of collateral: a full-blown tank farm of soy and cottonseed oil, the major use for which is salad oil. Tino had grand ambitions for his salad-oil business: He wanted to become the world's biggest distributor of salad oil, and to do so he needed loans. To get loans, he needed a field warehouse. So he turned to American Express Field Warehousing to help him out.

The field warehousing division was happy to give Tino a leg up, mainly because DeAngelis was a big customer, and the operation needed a few big customers. The top brass at American Express, unimpressed by the division's earnings, had been threatening to close down field warehousing since the ascendancy of Howard Clark to the head of Amex in 1960. Before then, field warehousing had been a pet project of Ralph Reed, American Express's former head honcho.

If American Express had closed down the field warehousing operation, it would have had little impact on the company. It would have had a big impact on Donald Miller, the head of American Express Field Warehousing, however, and he fought strenuously to keep it. So the arrival of Anthony DeAngelis, with his big tank farm in Bayonne, was fortuitous for Miller. With Tino at his side, Miller could point to a profitable operation—and a continued place in the American Express hierarchy.

There were some problems with taking on Tino as a client, however. For one thing, American Express didn't have anyone in the organization who was all that familiar with the salad-oil market, or the storage thereof. For another thing, there were some peculiarities about Tino's tank farm. First of all, Tino's employees lived awfully well, with some janitors and maintenance men making about $400 a week—heady salaries for unskilled laborers at the time. These highly compensated employees were also hired by American Express to look after the inventory. Tino, a rotund man who loved to be loved, thought the high salaries commanded loyalty, which they did. They also brought extreme cooperation in whatever Tino wanted done.

Another troubling aspect of the tank farm was the system of interconnecting pipes that ran underneath the tanks. American Express had taken note of them, but decided that pipes were secured against any oil being taken out of the tanks without notice.

As the 1960s dawned, Tino's star rose. First of all, he was doing a lively business in the salad-oil business, with some 65 million pounds of salad oil resting in his tanks. At 10 cents a pound, Tino's salad oil was worth about $6.5 million. Those sorts of figures command attention, which he got from banks and exporters as well.

Secondly, Tino had begun to realize that he could use his warehouse receipts for other purposes—such as playing the commodity futures markets. Commodities futures are contracts that require someone to buy or sell a set amount of goods at a set price at a specific time in the future. They're also one of the best ways to make or lose vast amounts of money in almost no time flat.

Oddly enough, futures have their origins not in gambling, but in reducing risk; and, for a major commodities dealer like Tino, a certain amount of playing the futures market would have been deemed prudent. Trading futures came into being because those who use raw materials often have to order them months in advance. Similarly, farmers like to know in advance what they'll get for their crops.

Suppose for example, Farmer Bill needs to get $1.00 a bushel for his wheat in the fall or he'll have to pull up stakes. The price of wheat is now $1.05 a bushel, but if there's a bumper harvest, the price will easily fall below $1.00. So Farmer Bill, who's outstanding in his field, makes an agreement with the local grain elevator operator: The operator will buy Bill's wheat for $1.00 a bushel, no matter what the prevailing price is at the time. If wheat falls below $1.00, the grain operator will take the loss; if wheat rises to $1.20 a bushel, the operator will make a tidy profit. In either case, Farmer Bill will live to plant another day.

The contract for future delivery—which is the proper name for a futures contract—can be sold to someone else, which is where the grain operator gets off the hook and the element of speculation comes in. Suppose, for example, the grain operator sells the contract to a dentist in Des Moines who thinks that the price of wheat will rise. The dentist, then, is obligated to take Farmer Bill's wheat and pay him $1.00 a bushel. If the price of wheat rises to, say, $1.10 a bushel, the dentist can take the wheat, resell it on the cash market, and make a dime per bushel in profit. If wheat falls to 90 cents per bushel, the dentist will have a 10-cent-per-bushel cavity to fill.

Modern futures trading is done on exchanges, which act to make sure there's a buyer for every seller and vice-versa. The exchanges also try, with occasional success, to keep shennanigans down to a minimum. Because buying and selling contracts is made so easy by the exchanges, however, you need only to put down a "good faith" deposit in order to trade contracts—that is, you can operate on margin, with the usual salutary or desultory results. In most cases, the margin deposit is about 10 percent of the contract. This means that if you agree to take delivery of a wheat contract for 5,000 bushels at $1.00 a bushel, you only have to put down $500 to control $5,000 of wheat. If wheat moves to $1.05 a bushel, you've doubled your money. If wheat sinks to 95 cents a bushel, you've crapped out.

Tino (remember Tino?) may have started out prudently in the futures markets, but he gave it up rather rapidly. His margin money for contracts as well as other ventures was financed by receipts from his Bayonne tank farm, as well as by willing lenders such as Continental Illinois and several British banks. As his need for cash grew, so did his commodities accounts at such major institutions as Ira Haupt & Company. And, in turn, as his commodities accounts grew, so did the inventory at the Bayonne tank plant.

From time to time after 1960, American Express as well as the several lenders involved grew a bit suspicious about all that salad oil in New Jersey. In many cases, Miller, not eager to anger DeAngelis, simply waved off the suspicions, declining to take any extra measures to make sure that all the salad oil was, in fact, in the tanks. From time to time, however, American Express would make an attempt to audit the Bayonne operation.

The audits were far from rigorous, however. In many cases, since Tino's well-paid employees were also lesser-paid employees of American Express, Allied Crude Vegetable Oil Refining Corporation seemed unusually well-prepared for what were supposed to be surprise visits. Everything seemed quite satisfactory at all the oil tanks whenever the inspectors came to visit. One reason for this may have been that those who did the actual measuring were Tino's employees—the inspectors allowed Tino's men to climb up to the top of the tanks, throw in the measuring lines, and sing out the tank levels.

Even if the inspectors had gone to the top of the tanks, however, it's doubtful they would have noticed anything unusual, unless they had planned to go snorkeling in the tanks. DeAngelis had latched onto a simple bit of chemistry that American Express had overlooked: Oil floats on top of water. And many of the tanks that looked like they were oil from the top were, in fact, several inches of salad oil covering many feet of water pumped in from the bottom. Tino's tank farm was worth only a fraction of what he—and American Express Field Warehousing—said it was, unless you happened to be a fish.

Just when Tino began filling his tanks with water isn't clear, but it was probably as early as 1960. At any rate, Allied Crude's inventory increased each year, sometimes at dizzying rates. By early 1963, Tino claimed to have over 800 million pounds of salad oil in his tanks—more than the entire U.S. production for the year. American Express officials, lulled by Tino's fat fees and having problems of their own with their travel card business, didn't bother to look too closely at the field warehousing operations.

One reason the top brass were unaware of any problems at the Bayonne tank farm was Thomas McLarney, the chief inspector of the Amex's field warehouse there. As the years went by, McLarney grew close to Tino and his men— uncomfortably close, in fact, since he participated in some of Tino's sideline businesses. McLarney wasn't alone, however: Donald Miller, the head of the division, found some of Tino's stock attractive as well.

Tino's investments, at this point, had grown quite large. With the receipts for over 800 million gallons of largely ficticious salad oil, Tino had become a major customer at Ira Haupt & Company. Although Haupt had a total capital of some $8 million, it had courteously arranged financing for Tino's speculations to the tune of $37 million. Haupt's basis for those efforts, of course, were the warehouse receipts furnished by American Express Field Warehousing. Several other smaller brokerage houses had also extended themselves, although not to the extent that Haupt & Company had.

As it turned out, 1963 was not to be Tino's year. For one thing, he'd decided to corner both the soy and cottonseed markets, a fairly lunatic decision. First of all, cornering both markets would probably require more capital than he had and would put his empire at considerable risk; second, the exchanges don't allow corners.

At this point, just about everyone began to get nervous about Tino. American Express, for example, began to wake up to the fact that if something went wrong at Bayonne, they could be liable for the millions in receipts they'd issued. Bankers began to realize that if the price of salad oil dipped significantly, the value of their collateral would fall below the value of credit they'd extended to Tino.

In November 1963, Amex, which had sold out all of its field warehousing operations except Tino's, decided to sell their business with Tino as well. This left Tino somewhat in the lurch, as it would be some time before the new outfit would be able to issue yet more warehouse receipts. In the meantime, Tino's salad-oil speculation was turning against him: He needed cash, and quickly, to raise his increasing margin calls at Haupt and elsewhere. For a while, he was able to make due by forging about $39 million of Amex receipts. Even that expedient didn't work for long, however; and, on November 18, 1963, Allied Crude Vegetable Oil Refining Corporation filed for bankruptcy.

During that week, things went from bad to worse for American Express, Haupt & Company, and the New York Stock Exchange. First of all, the magnitude of Tino's scam started becoming increasingly clear. Lawyers for Haupt presented warehouse receipts for $18 million to American Express officials, who pronounced them completely fraudulent. A judge ordered Amex to produce 160 million pounds of salad oil on behalf of an exporter; they were unable to do so. In fact, of the 900 million pounds of salad oil for which American Express Field Warehousing had issued receipts, less than one tenth—only 80 million—actually existed. The rest was water.

When word came out about Allied's bankruptcy, American Express stock wilted like lettuce. The potential losses for Amex could have totaled some $137 million, a sum that Amex would have found extremely difficult to raise. Even more disconcerting was the fact that Amex was one of the few joint-stock companies left on the Exchange. Way back in the 1850s, joint-stock companies were the norm, and American Express had never gotten around to changing their stock structure. The problem with joint-stock companies was that shareholders could be liable, without limit, for the company's losses. In other words, creditors could dun each and every American Express shareholder for the total amount of the company's liability in the salad-oil scandal.

Problems on the Exchange were just beginning, however. On Tuesday, a representative from Haupt & Company walked into the Exchange and informed it that the company was probably bankrupt. The next day, all Haupt accounts were frozen—that is, its 20,000 customers could neither buy stocks through Haupt nor sell the ones they had. Under the weight of Haupt's suspension—as well as the simultaneous suspension of Williston & Beane, which had another 9,000 customers—the stock market sank further.

Then, on Friday, November 22, 1963, John F. Kennedy was gunned down in Dallas. Stocks plunged at the news; and, as rumors flew, the plunge developed into a full-fledged panic, one of the worst in the Exchange's history. From 1:40 P.M., when the news of the events in Dallas reached the Exchange, to 2:07 P.M., when the president of the Exchange closed it down, the value of the stock market fell by $13 billion—the sharpest decline in the history of the Exchange.

By the end of the week, officials at the exchange realized just how much an erstwhile salad-oil king and a madman in Texas could affect their usually orderly realm. The stock market was in the throes of a panic, two brokerage houses were bankrupt, and one of the mightiest companies in America was embroiled in a potentially lethal scandal.

Over the weekend, the officials at the Exchange decided that something had to be done to bail out the 30,000 customers at Haupt & Company and Williston & Beane. A plan was quickly devised whereby the member firms of the Exchange, with the consent of the banks involved, would bail out the customers at the bankrupt firm.

This was an unprecedented move; in most cases, when a member went belly up, it was simply too bad. The customers took it on the chin along with the partners of the brokerage firm. This time, however, things were different. To allow the brokerages to fail would simply feed the panic, resulting in a crash that could rival 1929.

The lights burned around the clock on Wall Street that weekend as member firms bickered over who would pay what. The member firms, of course, wanted the Exchange to shoulder much of the tab; the Exchange had different ideas. Eventually it was decided that the Exchange would kick in up to $12 million, with a consortium of banks and brokerages throwing in the rest.

American Express, after a similar amount of agonized debate, also announced that it was willing to make good on its errors. This was a considerable feat for a corporation, even one of American Express's size: Although Amex carried insurance on its field warehousing operations, its losses could eventually have totaled over $100 million. Nevertheless, the company decided it had a moral obligation to make good on its mistakes.

For once—whether by chance or long experience with panics—Wall Street did the right thing. The announcement that Haupt and Williston & Beane's customers would be "made whole" calmed some of the panic on the Street. By the next year, the bull market had resumed, and the Dow Jones industrial average exceeded its 1963 highs. The Exchange's action eventually led to the formation of the Securities Investor Protection Corporation in 1970, which protects investors up to $500,000 per account in the event of a brokerage-house failure.

American Express's announcement calmed investors even more, although the stock would ultimately decline by 50 percent before recovering. Amex's handling of the affair, however, did the company worlds of good on the public-relations front.

As for Tino, his dreams of being the salad-oil king disappeared. So did he. He served 7 years of a 20-year sentence for fraud, with the small consolation of becoming a minor celebrity. As much as Tino had failed, he had succeeded in doing one thing: duping one of the largest corporations in America.

THE MAN WHO PUT THE BULL IN BULLION

David Allan Saxon had discovered a foolproof way to buy gold.[1]

Gold has several problems as an investment: It's too heavy to cart around with you, people like to steal it, and the price goes down.[2]

Many people who really, really like gold have found ways to safeguard it. Unfortunately, most of these ways involve living like animals far off in the countryside and shooting at neighbors with assault weapons.[3]

Naturally, this sort of behavior scares off the average investor, who might want to include a bit of gold in his or her portfolio as a hedge against inflation. Saxon realized this and created North American Bullion Reserves.

---

[1]Well, almost.
[2]As it has, on balance, since 1980.
[3]When civilization collapses, though, they'll get to laugh.

The concept was simple: Buy your gold through North American, get a receipt, and your gold will be stored in a Utah depository. No muss, no fuss.[4]

The idea was so good that several prominent gold gurus, such as Howard Ruff, recommended North American to their investors. The system apparently worked well for a while.[5]

The main problem with the scheme was that Saxon had two very large character faults. The first was that he enjoyed the trappings of wealth, like Maseratis and San Diego beach houses. The second was that he fancied himself a sharp futures trader.[6]

By most accounts, Saxon wasn't a bad fellow.[7] The temptation of the money that poured into North American, however, was too much for him. In order to buy the things he wanted, he had to earn some extra money; and, since most people didn't drop by to visit their gold, he used most of it to trade gold futures.[8]

By and by, people became suspicious. Howard Ruff, whose investors had put some $12 million into North American, told them to pull out—which they did. North American complied, but the strain was too much on the company. Some $60 million disappeared into thin air.[9]

---

[4]You could even go look at it if you wanted to.

[5]As long as too many people didn't go to look at their gold.

[6]He made one or two sharp trades, but those didn't quite make up for the dozens of really bad ones.

[7]With the possible exceptions of the accounts of the thousands of people who bought gold from him.

[8]Unfortunately, he lost most of it.

[9]Saxon was able to salt away a few krugerrands in the trunk of his Maserati.

The company, which advertised "Gold You Can Fold and Take with You," folded under the weight of a New York State audit. Saxon committed suicide, and gold investors remain stuck with gold in their possession.[10]

AFTERWORD

Many panics are the result of large, long-term economic effects that build up over the years like hot lava under a volcano. Others, however, are the result of a single, devastating blow to the system. The death of John F. Kennedy was one of the latter. His assasination in Dallas led to one of the sharpest single losses in stock market history.

What shook the system just as much, however, were the failures of several large commodities dealers that had been taken in by a small con man with large dreams. Although the stock market recovered, the great salad oil caper shook the financial system to its very roots.

The salad oil caper illustrates one aspect of a theory that's currently in great vogue among market experts. The theory is chaos theory, which argues that large, complex systems have relatively simple laws that produce unpredictible effects. One upshot of the theory is that very small things can have very great effects, somewhat like the old science fiction stories where a time traveler disturbs a small object in his journey, resulting in the loss of World War II by the Allies. Scientists call this the butterfly effect, where, theoretically, the beating of a butterfly's wings could ultimately lead to a hurricane.

---

[10]The system has its flaws, but at least you know where it is.

Whatever the true meaning—if any—behind the forces that shape the stock market, the salad oil episode shows the dangers of taking anyone at face value when large sums of money are at stake. Indeed, one of the more remarkable aspects of high finance is that the greater the sum of money involved, the more casual the participants tend to be. A bank that would turn down a $100,000 mortgage because of several late bills will often lend millions on a handshake to a developer with a flashy history.

The major source for this episode is Norman Miller, *The Wall Street Journal* reporter who covered the story as it unfolded. His book, *The Great Salad Oil Swindle,* is a wonderful account of Tino DeAngelis's rise to salad oil immortality and provides wonderful details of Tino's little empire. Peter Grossman's history of American Express provides fascinating details of how the company got itself into such a messy deal.

SELECTED BIBLIOGRAPHY

Grossman, Peter Z. *American Express: The Unofficial History of the People Who Built the Great Financial Empire.* New York: Crown Publishers, Ltd., 1987.
Miller, Norman, *The Great Salad Oil Swindle.* New York: Coward McCann, 1965.

CHAPTER 7

HOW TO AVOID BEING IN THE SEQUEL TO THIS BOOK

"Son, I've got some advice for you. Have a seat. When I was your age, I took all my hard-earned cash and invested it in a rip-roaring proposition that was all the rage those days. No one warned me about the risks: Everyone else was doing it, so I did it too. And you know what? I made a bundle. Enough to retire at 33. Kept every cent of it, too, and now I sleep on a bed of crisp hundred-dollar bills that I give to the poor when it gets wrinkled. Now, here's a whole wad of cash—go invest in whatever everyone else does, and you'll do just fine."

If your parents told that to you, you're probably the only one. Most people get treated to long, tedious lectures stressing the virtue of hard work, of slow, careful thrift, and the value of money. The tradition stretches back hundreds of years. It may be genetic. Think back on the line, "Neither a borrower nor a lender be." Sound familiar? It's from *Hamlet,* but just about everyone has heard it from some sanctimonious relative or friend at one time or another, usually when they're turning you down for a loan. Don't blame Shakespeare for espousing that viewpoint, however—he put it in the mouth of Polonious, a tiresome old fool whose platitudes were chestnuts back in the 16th century.

It would be easy to dismiss all those who have been caught up in manias, panics and frauds as silly, greedy people. In fact, that's usually what everyone does, once something particularly big and bad happens in the financial world. After the stock market crash of 1987, for example, the news was filled with gleeful market reporters telling of the market's headlong rush to disaster. The same was true in 1929 and, for that matter, in 1836. The forecasters were different each time, but the message was the same: "Jerks. I told you so."

In truth, only a very few ever do predict crashes. In 1987, of all the market timers tracked by the *Hulbert Financial Digest,* one of the more prominent newsletters that keeps tabs of market timers' recommendations, only three forecasters cashed in their followers' chips in time. One of them, Robert Prechter, editor of the *Eliott Wave Theorist,* did so by default. Prechter, who had forecast that the Dow would peak somewhere around 3,600, had told his investors that the market's October weakness was a good opportunity to buy. Prudently, however, he'd also recommended they put in a "stop-loss" order at a lower level. A stop-loss order tells your broker to sell you out when the market hits a certain level, thereby keeping your losses to a minimum. On October 16, 1987, the last trading day before the crash, Prechter's followers were stopped out of the market. Another of the timers who got out in time based his prediction on the fact that there was a lunar eclipse over New York that weekend.

Only a very few were actually out of the stock market on October 19, 1987, when the Dow fell 508 points—the biggest point decline in history. Even fewer took what would have been the best play that day, which was to sell stocks short and buy bonds. The managers of the nation's mutual funds and pension funds—again with a few exceptions—were on the wrong side of the market on Black Monday. The best and brightest minds in the brokerage industry watched in horror as their carefully planned "portfolio insurance" programs, highly sophisticated hedging operations using futures and options, actually fanned the flames of the stock market meltdown. The big guys, the "smart money," fared no better than the little guys.

So if you think that financial catastrophes only happen to other people, you're probably due for a rude awakening at some point in your life. Every market—stocks, bonds, gold, commodities, and real estate—gets slapped into the tank at some point or another. Even ultrasafe Treasury bills and certificates of deposit wind up on the losing end occasionally, if only due to inflation. And the most prudent people can get stung by con artists.

This doesn't mean that you should stuff your mattress with your savings and surround yourself with Rottweilers and howitzers, either. What you should do, however, is acquaint yourself with some of the signposts of manias and frauds—and make sure that if either strikes, you've got money in other places that will help make up the losses.

Let us take up the issue of manias and panics first. The signs of a true money mania are legion, but they're often discovered after the fact. This is one of those annoying things about life, like the fact that eating several pounds of cookies a day makes you fat. Nevertheless, one of the first characteristics of a mania—in fact, virtually the definition of one—is that an awful lot of people are caught up in it, and, at the time, these people feel that they're not being particularly crazy.

Just why people behave this way is unclear, and people throughout the ages have devised theories about it, ranging from sheer randomness to the majestic movements of the stars through the heavens. No one has come up with a reliable system for predicting manias. Sir Isaac Newton, no dummy, pondered the question after losing 20,000 pounds in a stock scheme. "I can calculate the motions of the heavenly bodies," he commented, "but not the madness of people."

Even if you can't predict manias and the panics that usually follow in their wakes, you can keep an eye open and be aware when they're happening. Perhaps the best method is to watch mob psychology. Keep in mind, however, that there are two mobs to watch: the general public and the Wall Street pros. According to hoary financial wisdom, the most dangerous time is when the bootless and unhorsed get into the act. In reality, however, the most dangerous time is when the professionals get overly excited about the market.

Wall Street professionals look down on the populace partly because the so-called "little guy" doesn't have market savvy and, at least in the past, has tended to jump in just before the whole shebang goes down the tubes. This, in fact, has been true in the past and particularly during the 1929 stock market mania, when investors bought just about any of the shamelessly overpriced stocks, bonds, and mutual funds that Wall Street produced. One suspects that the other reason Wall Street pros look down on the little guy is because they can't find anyone else greedier than they are.

If you want to measure public sentiment, one of the best methods is to watch the daily newscasts and read the weekly newsmagazines, like *Time* and *Newsweek*. In journalism, business writing is a small, odd enclave that, in most journalists' eyes, is one step up from writing obituaries. Business editors, most times, have to fight to get their stories on the front page. The reason is that for readers a story on IBM's earnings or the gross national product is about as interesting as spending an evening with an insurance salesman.

When stories about the stock market, or commercial property, or any other financial subject, for that matter, begin to take up prime time on the evening news or prime space on the cover of a big news magazine, you should approach that market like you would a pit bull on crack. When a really big market opportunity does come, it's unlikely you're going to get your tip from Peter Jennings or Dan Rather.

If you keep your eyes open, you can see other signs. Do there seem to be an inordinate number of real estate agents around? Do the people who work on Wall Street seem unusually young and inexcusably rich? Do you notice an awful lot of chatter at parties about precious metals, commodities, tax shelters, mutual funds? If so, be on your guard. It may be a sign that a mania is in progress. On the other hand, it might also be a sign that you hang out with really dull people.

You can use more concrete ways of measuring popular sentiment, however. The oldest—and probably least accurate—measure can be found in "odd-lot activity," a figure that's generally reported daily by the New York Stock Exchange. Odd lots are stock purchases less than 100 shares (100-share purchases are called "round lots"). When odd-lot purchases increase, it's a sign the small investor is hopping on the bandwagon. That, in turn, is a sign to be wary of the stock market. When odd-lot short sales increase, it means that the small investor is betting the market will fall—in which case the prudent course of action is to buy.

The problem with this measure is that most small speculators don't buy stocks. They buy stock options, which are both cheaper and riskier. Options have been around for a long time. One of the earliest forms of the stock option appeared in Holland in the 1600s, in the midst of one of that country's many investment manias during the 17th and 18th centuries. The Dutch word for options trading, *Windhandel,* translates to "trading air"—and it's an apt one.

An option is the right, but not the obligation, to buy stock at a set price by a set date. For example, an option might give the holder the right to buy 100 shares of Amalgamated MooseMobile at $20 per share within the next three months. In most cases, buying the option is far cheaper than buying the stock itself—about $2 to $15 per option—hence one of its appeals to investors. If you play the game and win, you can make big profits, because the option will give you much larger gains than the stock will. Naturally, the reverse is true, too. What's more, you don't have the luxury of time if you pick a losing option, nor do you get the benefits of dividends or splits. If you don't have a winner in three months, you're out.

You can get a feel for the options market sentiment by looking at the put-to-call ratio. In the options market, you buy a put when you're bearish, and you buy a call when you're bullish. If you just want to make a bet on the direction of the stock market, you buy puts or calls on the Standard & Poor's 100 option, which represents a basket of 100 of the stock market's leaders. The S&P 100 option is also known by its ticker symbol, the OEX.

Speculators, whether they're small investors or big players, tend to be an optimistic bunch, and there's usually more calls purchased than puts. Nevertheless, a put-to-call level of more than 1.2 calls to every put is usually a good indicator of frothy bullishness, and a put-to-call level of .7 calls to every put is a good indication of overwhelming bearishness. In short, you should be cautious buying when the options crowd is bullish, and you should reconsider selling when the options crowd is bearish.

In recent years, however, the best indication of stock market sentiment has been Wall Street itself. The reason is this: Picking stocks lost a great deal of popularity with the public during the 1973 to 1974 bear market, and individuals, as a whole, have been net sellers of individual stocks since then. The majority of cash in the market is run by the big guys—pension fund managers, mutual fund managers, and other large, institutional investors.

By necessity, the majority must be on the wrong side of the trade at the top of the market; that is, they must be buyers when the market peaks and sellers when the market bottoms. In the stock market crash of 1987, the majority buying at the top were the Wall Street professionals. A poll of big-money advisors taken by *Investors Intelligence,* an investment newsletter, revealed record bullishness in August 1987 —the top of the great 1982 to 1987 bull market. The same poll revealed record bearishness at the bottom of the market in December of that year. If you're still not convinced of the "odd-lotter" status of the big guys, consider this: Some 80 percent of all mutual-fund managers, theoretically the cream of Wall Street's investment advisors, underperform the Standard & Poor's index of 500 common stocks.

So how do you find out what the herd on the Street is thinking? One way is to look at the *Investors Intelligence* poll, which appears every week in *Barron's.* When more than 60 percent of the advisors are bullish, you should think twice about investing in the market. When fewer than 30 percent are bullish, think about buying. *Barron's* also carries advisory sentiment indexes on bonds and gold, carried out in this case by *The Bullish Consensus,* another investment newsletter.

Real estate is a different matter. You can use a two-pronged test for commercial real estate, the preferred vehicle for investors. First of all, take a look at local vacancy rates, which your local paper should be able to tell you. Are they rising or falling? If they're falling, then the local real estate scene might be a good idea. If they're rising, take a drive around town. How many new office buildings are under construction? If office buildings are beginning to sprout like dandelions on a spring lawn and vacancy rates are rising, it's probably wise to abandon the idea of investing in yet another one.

Big price increases, of course, are another hallmark of a mania. In a true mania, the surge in prices not only commands attention in and of itself, but it makes it almost physically painful not to be in on the action. Skeptics have to pay dearly, at least in emotional terms, for not investing.

The question here becomes how to gage what's a big price rise and what isn't. In markets where you can find prices accurately, which is to say in markets where items are priced daily, such as gold, commodities, stocks, and bonds, there are a few relatively simple methods. The first is to gage annual price increases against a relatively risk-less benchmark. The magnitude of the spread between the riskless return and the risky return will give you some idea of just how far out of whack any given market is.

The best benchmark for a riskless return is the one-year Treasury bill. These securities are about the safest thing you can buy, provided you hold them for the full year. The reason: They're backed by the full faith and credit of the U.S. government. Given the government's ongoing fiscal crises, you may snicker. Nevertheless, the government is obliged to pay off the people who hold Treasury securities before they pay anyone else, including insured bank depositors. There's something to be said for being at the head of the creditors' line.

You can find the yield on one-year T-bills in just about any newspaper in the world, even the East Podunk *Post*. Say, for example, that one-year T-bills are yielding 7.5 percent. That's the rate you get for taking no risk whatsoever, with the exception of tying up your cash for a year. If you hold on to your T-bill, it's pretty much a dead certainty that you'll get your principal and your 7.5 percent. And, even in the bleak possibility that the government defaults on its obligations and the world sinks into financial oblivion, you'll be about as well off as anyone else.

Now, supposing you note that the stock market has been rising at a 9 percent rate, which is its historical average over the last 60 years. Those extra 1.5 percentage points are your reward for braving the possibility that the market will go colder than last week's tuna casserole. You note, also, that home prices have been rising at a 20 percent clip over the past two years. That 20 percent increase is a sore temptation—but it's also a risky proposition. You're getting 12.5 percentage points more than you would from a riskless deal, which should indicate to you that you're taking a considerable amount of risk, particularly if you're playing the game with 10 percent down.

Sheer percentage gains over a year are also a measure in and of themselves. In the stock market, for example, a 30 percent annual gain is about as good as life gets. Jumping into the market when it's already risen by that much is asking for trouble. In the bond market, a 20 percent gain is reason to uncork the champagne. At the height of the junk-bond craze in the late 1980s, investors were reaping 30 percent or more on selected junk, and some 16 percentage points of that was from the bonds' yields alone. Some of those bonds ultimately yielded a great deal more, but no one was cheering: When a bond's yield goes up, its price goes down, and many of those invested in junk bonds reaped a bitter harvest. The gold market is somewhat more mercurial, as it were, but jumps of 30 percent or more should be treated with great caution, at least as far as buying opportunities go.

It should be noted that as a mania progresses and prices seem high to even the experts, you'll note a change in the way people talk about high prices. At this point the most dangerous four words in finance appear: "This time it's different." During the stock market mania of the 1920s, for example, perfectly sensible and respectable people believed that the stock market and the economy had entered a new period of prosperity. Depressions were obsolete; the stock market was a vehicle by which everyone could, and should, become a millionaire. As late as 1926, the final year of the Florida land boom, people wrote essays in respectable economic magazines arguing that there was no boom in land prices in Florida—they were simply catching up to their true worth. Needless to say, when you see such tracts in defense of insane price increases, you should be especially wary.

Another touchstone of manias is the proliferation of ways for people to play the game. When the housing market is red hot, for instance, you see ads mentioning creative financing, because the cost of housing is out of reach for most people. In some cases, these methods are truly innovative and help people get into homes they couldn't otherwise afford. In other cases, they simply help people get much further over their heads than they ordinarily could.

If you're a real estate buff, another signpost to look at is what bankers are touting as the hottest area in banking. Usually, this is accompanied by large-scale whining about government regulations and unfair competition. As a general rule of thumb, whatever banks are extremely interested in this year will be next year's financial crisis. If the hottest topic is real estate, consider renting for a few years. Tracking bank interest isn't easy, but a weekly sampling of such publications as *American Banker* and *The Wall Street Journal* will give you a good idea.

In the stock market, you'll notice a proliferation of "derivative instruments"—proxies for the stock market, in other words. In most cases, these are ways you can lose money far more quickly than you could in the market itself. Once again, the options market is a handy indicator. Inevitably, you'll see the options market get more attention during a roaring bull market. In 1987, the options market went wild, with new options combinations appearing regularly. You could even get options on futures contracts, which is somewhat like betting on the outcome of another bet.

Mutual funds still tend to proliferate during a mania and probably always will. For example, at the beginning of 1989, there was only one closed-end mutual fund that restricted its investments to West German stocks: The Germany Fund. The fund was buoyed by hopeful developments for the formation of a unified Europe in 1992, as well as the collapse of the Berlin Wall, and was one of the top stocks for the year. By June of 1990, Wall Street had rolled out another seven German funds. As a result, demand for the original Germany fund evaporated, and the stock remained in the doldrums for the rest of the year.

Frauds are another matter entirely. People love to read about financial frauds for the same reason people love to read about sordid romances: It's nice to know that you haven't taken leave of your senses, or at least you haven't been caught.

But fraud is no laughing matter. Even the simplest scam is hard to detect. What's more, once a fraud is uncovered, the money is usually long gone. Although Americans seem to have a soft spot for con artists, those who engage in financial larceny rarely steal from the rich. The best targets are the proverbial widows and orphans—those whose life savings are on the line. Whether they invest because they're gullible, unwary, or desperate to increase what little cash they have, the consequences for them is often a diminished life. A retirement in poverty is far too harsh a punishment for being a victim.

Although frauds are perennial problems, they flourish during boom times. In fact, a rise in fraud in any given market is a sign that that market is in the midst of a mania. When ordinary investments give outlandish returns, outlandish investments seem more ordinary. Frauds are, in one sense, simply woof to a mania's warp.

For example, in the early 1980s in Phoenix, Arizona, one of the most harebrained investment schemes in the world came to light. A financial planner came to his clients with the documentation for a limited partnership. This in itself was not unusual. Planners at the time were crazy about partnerships, primarily because of the fat commissions they generated.

This particular planner had an investment that rang nearly every bell an investor could possibly have. The planner told his clients that a company he was aware of, Rex Rabbit, was using genetic engineering (biotechnology!) to develop (research and development tax credits!!) a new strain of rabbit. The rabbit was an improvement on an existing breed, the Rex Rabbit, which is a big bunny indeed. This "super rabbit" would not only have luxuriant pelts, but be tasty as well (big profits!!!).

Not only was this company close to achieving its goal, he told them, but it had already lined up contracts with major New York furriers for the rabbit pelts (Big Apple cash!!!!). The best is yet to come, he whispered: The company also had a contract in the works to sell the meat to the South Korean mercenaries who guarded the Saudi royal family (petrodollars!!!!!). A substantial investment now, the planner assured his clients, would reap big benefits soon.

Stupid? Yes. But the planner pulled in an average of $27,000 apiece from 40 investors, for a total of over $1 million. Needless to say, he wasn't able to pull the rabbit out of his hat, and his investors were hopping mad. But he had pushed enough hot buttons—enough mania buzzwords—to pull in over a million dollars.

The first rule in avoiding being stung, of course, is to adhere to the basic rule of investing, which is to treat everyone with deep-seated suspicion. Your sainted mother may love you, but she may also love Brazil. You may have known your broker since you were toddlers, but that's no reason to hand over investment money without a written agreement, and preferably one written by your attack dog of a lawyer. A good con artist goes for a sure thing, and one of the surest things is someone filled with good will and trust.

So start by looking at an investment with the same sort of wary eye you'd use when buying a car. When you go to buy a car, you generally don't look at the car salesman as someone with your best interests in mind. Granted, you have similar goals: You want to buy a car, and he wants to sell you one. When you go to invest, you share the same convergence of interests: You want to buy something—an investment—and the person on the other end of the deal wants to sell you one.

There the similarities end, of course. A salesman's goal is to make money. Good salesmen realize that gouging a customer will ultimately result in less business down the road, but it's a large act of charity to believe that all salesmen have your best interests at heart. The heart of any transaction—in cars or investments—is money; and where your money is involved, you should be wary.

You should be particularly wary of anyone peddling investments whom you don't know, or haven't had recommended to you. The basic investment scam revolves around high-pressure telephone sales. You get a call from a broker. He's got a hot investment—in East German banks, orange juice futures, high-technology stocks, what have you. Invest now, the con artist says, and you'll make more money than you can imagine. Hesitate, and the opportunity is lost. Send that check now, and you'll be wealthy beyond your wildest dreams.

It's surprising how many people fall for these kinds of pitches every day. No matter how appealing the sales pitch may be, think how you'd react if you'd gotten the same call from a car salesman. "Mr. Bing, I've got a dandy MooseMobile right here in the showroom. It's got climate control, cruise control, noise control, and pollution control. The MooseMobile goes from 0 to 100 in 50 seconds, and it gets 300 miles to the gallon. The driver's seat has electric massage, and the trunk will fit a peck of pachyderms. Just send me a check for $20,000, and it's yours."

Naturally, you wouldn't buy a car sight-unseen. You shouldn't consider an investment, sight-unseen, either. If your curiosity is piqued by a broker's cold call, start asking for some specifics. Kick the tires a bit, as it were. If the broker's selling a stock, ask for a prospectus and an annual report. And don't be satisfied if you get an official-looking document in the mail. Read it. The prospectus should tell you, for example, who the company's management is and how much experience they have in their line of business. It will tell you if there are any lawsuits against the company as well as what the company's assets are. The prospectus will also tell you how the company plans to use the proceeds of the stock sale if it is a new offering.

A variation of the sight-unseen investment is the delayed-delivery investment, usually precious metals. The pitch here is fairly simple: "Send us your money now, and we'll give you a discount on the price of gold, provided you just wait a few months before we deliver it." The odds are overwhelming that the deal is bogus. By the time your delivery date rolls around, your gold dealer is long gone and so is your cash.

This scam has been around so long it's astonishing, and it works almost every time. The most spectacular use of this scam was with the International Gold Bullion Exchange, which promised investors low prices on precious metals—provided IGBE stored the metal for them. The company racked up $300 million in sales from 250,000 investors across the country before investigators decided to open up IGBE's vaults and have a peek. They found 40 bars of gold, which, on closer inspection, turned out to be wooden blocks painted yellow. All the rest of the cash was gone, spent mainly on the high living of the company's officers. In the case of gold, the rule is this: If you're crazy, deal with an out-of-state dealer you've never heard of. If you're really crazy, ask them to store it for you.

Even if you're dealing with someone you think is a legitimate broker, be sure to ask that any documentation is sent to you via the U.S. mail. The reason: Sending documents through the mails puts you under the protection of the U.S. Postal Service. You may snicker when you hear that, but the U.S. Postal Inspectors, who investigate mail fraud, are the best-kept secret in law enforcement. Their record at catching con artists—or anyone else, for that matter—is better than the FBI's. And there's nothing that warms a postal inspector's heart more than an envelope from a con artist with a stamp on it.

Con artists know about the Postal Service's efficiency, of course, which is why they're so fond of doing business by phone. If the broker on the other end of the deal balks at sending documents through the mail, wash your hands of the whole deal. If they offer to send it Federal Express, decline politely and ask for Express Mail. Be sure to keep any documents you get.

Even if you do get an authentic-looking prospectus through the mail, you still have some work to do. Take the time to investigate the people offering the investment. It doesn't take long to call the Better Business Bureau, the Securities and Exchange Commission, the National Association of Securities Dealers, or the North American Association of Securities Administrators, all of whom can tell you whether the company you're dealing with has a satisfactory record of dealing with investors. That time could be money in the bank—and out of a ripoff artist's hands.

If all of this sounds like a lot of work, it is. But when push comes to shove, the job of protecting your cash is up to you. Most of us were brought up with the impression that the government had a vast army of people watching out for the consumer, protecting us from false advertising, shady dealers, and criminals. That impression, unfortunately, is wrong.

The truth of the matter is that federal regulatory agencies are understaffed and hopelessly outnumbered. If you don't think so, consider this: According to various estimates, some $200 to $400 billion disappeared during the savings and loan crisis. The reason—aside from monumental greed and stupidity—was that federal regulators simply couldn't keep up. By the time most S&Ls were declared insolvent, they had been so for a long time. And bad loan portfolios don't improve with age.

Other agencies are similarly strapped. The Securities and Exchange Commission, the federal watchdog that oversees brokerage activities, has been running at low staffing levels for some time. For example, the staff that oversees mutual funds has remained the same size since 1980 —even though the mutual-fund industry has grown tenfold. What's more, since the government must adhere to an equitable pay scale, the SEC must pay workers in New York and San Francisco the same amount they pay investigators in Peoria. Try raising a family in New York City on $35,000 a year.

Where federal regulators fail, state regulators attempt to fill the gap—and they do heroic work. By necessity, however, their efforts must be somewhat piecemeal, as each state has different views on securities law. And even though their association, the North American Securities Administrators Association, works hard at exposing frauds and proposing uniform laws, it's all uphill work.

Even if you do luck out and the bad guys are caught, don't think that you'll see any of your money back. Securities enforcers' first goal is to stop illegal practices; making the victims whole again has to take a back seat. In most cases, when you've been stung, your money is long gone. Suing the bastards won't bring it back and neither will a court of law.

So when dealing with your money, it's best to be careful. Manias and frauds have been around for a long time, and they'll be here a long time after we've cashed that Big Check in the Sky. The odds are good that at some time in your life, you'll get caught up in a panic or robbed by a con artist. What is there to do? Not much—except to be careful and never put too much into any one investment.

INDEX